The Big Book of

Horse Trivia

for Kids

Fun Facts and Stories about Ponies, Horses, and the Equestrian Lifestyle

Bernadette Johnson

T0017509

BLOOM BOOKS
FOR YOUNG READERS

Published by:
Bloom Books for Young Readers,
an imprint of Ulysses Press
PO Box 3440
Berkeley, CA 94703
www.ulyssespress.com

ISBN: 978-1-64604-447-4
Library of Congress Control Number: 2022944105

Printed in the United States
10 9 8 7 6 5 4 3 2 1

Acquisitions editor: Claire Sielaff
Managing editor: Claire Chun
Editor: Lauren Schiffman
Proofreader: Joyce Wu
Front cover design: Ashley Prine
Cover and interior art: Andy Robbins
Interior design and layout: Winnie Liu
Cover art: from shutterstock.com—icon above title © Enola99d; horse
    © Andrew Shevchuk; objects © Sunshine Vector
Interior art: from shutterstock.com—chapter opening pages
    © SunshineVector; horseshoe bullets © WarmWorld; page 11 horse
    © LynxVector

IMPORTANT NOTE TO READERS: Although the author and publisher have made every effort to ensure that the information in this book was correct at press time, the author and publisher do not assume and hereby disclaim any liability to any party for any loss, damage, or disruption caused by errors or omissions, whether such errors or omissions result from negligence, accident, or any other cause.

To Jeffie, our furry canine companion Molly, and all the horses I've met over the years.

And to Ulysses, the pretty Bright Bay Morgan Breyer horse toy that lives on my desk as a reminder to keep going.

Contents

Chapter 2 It's Not Rocket Science: Horse Science and Biology...22

Chapter 3 Eat like a Horse: Feeding and Care 45

Chapter 5 Work Horses: Jobs for Equines and Their People 69

Chapter 6 The Inside Track: Horses in Sports and Show 76

Chapter 7 The Horse and Buggy Days: History of the Horse 89

Chapter 8 Horseplay: Arts, Entertainment, and Toys 106

Chapter 9 You Can Lead a Horse to Water: Horse-Related Sayings 117

Chapter 10 A Horse of a Different Color: Bonus Horse Facts 128

Introduction

Horses are noble, majestic, intelligent creatures who have served as workers and companions to humans for thousands of years. But what do we know about them? The answer is a lot! And you can too! Whether you are a horse fan, a budding equestrian (horse rider), or just curious, this trivia book will increase your horse sense with fun facts about our hoofed, four-legged friends and the ways they've changed our lives over the ages.

Horses have played a key role not only in meeting the farming and transportation needs of a great many people, but also in developing civilization, changing national boundaries, and spreading languages and mixing cultures all over the world. Warhorses, plow horses, and carriage horses have worked alongside people since we domesticated them—or trained wild horses to live and work with us. And since then, people have bred horses for certain traits. So now, much like dogs, there are hundreds of horse breeds with diverse features and abilities. These range from adorable miniature horses and ponies to huge draft horses and everything in between.

Although we don't need horses as much for pulling plows and carriages, horses still hold a place in the lives and hearts of many people. Horse lovers can participate in equestrian shows, horse races, rodeos, and other horse-driven entertainment. And you don't need to have your own horse to find opportunities to hang out with and ride horses through lessons and rentals at many stables and ranches. Some horses still pull not only carriages but barges. And, like dogs and other smaller animals, therapy horses are now a thing.

Here you can find out about horse biology, horse riding, horse jobs, horse sports, horse history, horse toys, and horses in general. You'll also learn sayings taken from the world of horses—right from the horse's mouth, so to speak.

No matter your equine (horse-related) experience level, you are bound to find juicy tidbits you didn't know about horses (and related animals) in these pages. Hopefully, this is a jumping off point to a wealth of newfound equestrian knowledge—and a fun read!

So get in the saddle, take the reins, and mosey through this book to discover a lot of cool facts about tons of horse-related topics.

Vocabulary
at a Glance

bit: a piece of material put in a horse's mouth that the reins attach to (see "reins" further down)

breed: (noun) a horse with certain traits and parentage; (verb) to have two horses mate and make baby horses

bridle: a harness that goes over a horse's head that the bit and reins are attached to

cavalry: soldiers who ride horses into battle

crossbreed: mating two horses of different types together to make babies who are a combination of the two

domestic/domesticated: trained to live and work alongside people

draft: also spelled draught, a word to describe horses who pull carts or equipment

dressage: dance-like moves that some horses and riders do in competitions

equestrian: a horse rider, and a word to describe anything to do with horse riding

equine: anything related to horses or their relatives—donkeys and zebras

feral: breeds that have never been domesticated

foal: a baby horse

gait: the way a horse walks

groom: to clean and brush a horse or other animal

mare: a female adult horse

reins: straps used by a rider to tell a horse which way to go

stable: a building where horses live and sleep

stallion: a male horse that is able to breed

stirrup: loops that a horse rider puts their feet in

tack: equipment that is put on a horse, like saddles, bridles, and reins

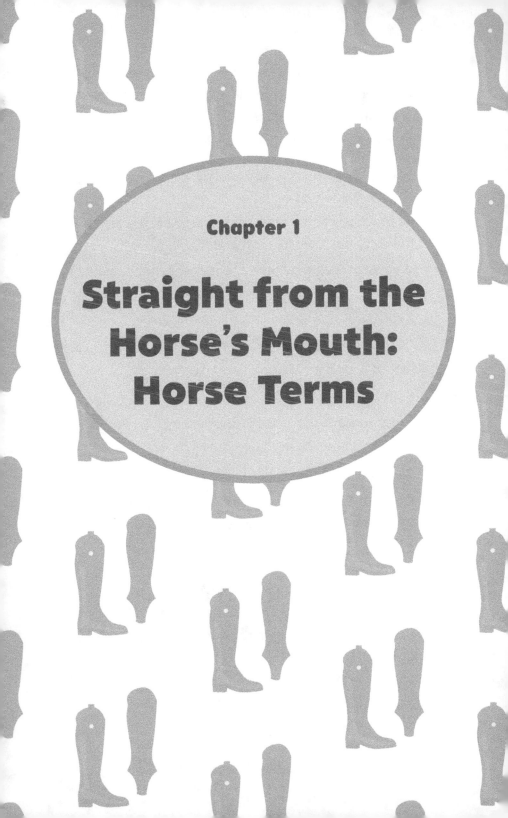

Chapter 1

Straight from the Horse's Mouth: Horse Terms

What does the word equestrian mean?

Equestrian can be used as an adjective to describe anything related to horse riding, like equestrian events or equestrian clothing. It can also be used as a noun to mean someone who rides horses. Are you a budding equestrian?

What are the terms for horses of different ages and genders?

- **Foal:** A baby horse of either sex that is still nursing (drinking milk from its mother)
- **Weanling:** A young horse of either sex that is no longer nursing
- **Yearling:** A 1-year-old horse of either sex
- **Colt:** A young male horse up to 3 years old
- **Filly:** A young female horse up to 3 years old
- **Mare:** An adult female horse
- **Broodmare:** A mare used for breeding
- **Dam:** The mother of a foal
- **Sire:** The father of a foal
- **Gelding:** A male horse that has gone through an operation so he can no longer breed
- **Stallion:** A male horse that is able to breed

What is a group of horses called?

Just like with cattle, a group of horses is called a herd. Horses are social animals, and they like to hang out in a herd full of their family and friends.

What is a green horse?

No, it's not a horse that's the color green. A green horse is one that is not very experienced or has very little training. In other words, it's not the best match for a green rider.

What are a horse's withers?

The withers are the top of a horse's shoulders, all the way up on its back (the top of the horse). When people want to find out a horse's height, they measure from the bottom of its front hooves (where they touch the ground) to its withers, rather than to the top of the head like you would be measured. So horses stand even taller than their measured heights when they raise their heads.

What unit of measurement is used to describe the height of a horse?

The hand is a unit of measurement used to measure a horse's height from hooves to withers (top of the shoulders). A hand used to be the actual width of a person's hand, but everyone's hands are different sizes. So to standardize the measurement, Henry VIII, king of England from 1491 to 1547, passed a law making the standard hand measure 4 inches. If you see a horse height of 15hh, that means 15 hands high. To translate to inches, just multiply 15 hands by 4 inches (the standard hand measurement). So a 15hh horse is 60 inches tall from hooves to withers. To translate to feet, divide the inches by 12. Sixty inches is 5 feet, so a 15hh horse is 5 feet tall.

What is a horse breed?

A breed is a group of horses that share ancestors and usually have common traits that are recognized as being typical for that type. The word breed is also used as a verb to describe horses mating to produce babies. People have been cross-breeding horses to favor certain traits for thousands of years. As a result, there are hundreds of breeds today that differ in size, appearance, personality, and a number of other features. Some popular breeds are Thoroughbred, Arabian, and Shetland pony.

Is a pony a baby horse?

No, pony doesn't mean baby horse (although baby ponies are technically baby horses too). Pony is a word used for breeds of horses that, as adults, average less than 14.2 hands high from the ground to their withers (top of the shoulders). That's around 57 inches, or nearly 5 feet tall. That's still taller than most kids!

What is a miniature horse?

Miniature horse breeds are even smaller than pony breeds, measuring less than 9.5 hands high. That is only 38 inches, or a little over 3 feet high. That's a little shorter than the Great Dane named Zeus whom Guinness World Records reported as the world's tallest dog in 2022 at 41.18 inches tall.

What is a studbook?

A studbook, sometimes also called a breed registry, is the official record of the pedigree, or ancestors, of horses that belong to a particular breed. Horse breeders began making them in the 1700s. One example is the *General Stud Book* of Thoroughbreds created in 1791 by James Weatherby.

What is a horse whose parents are unknown called?

A horse that isn't purebred, or whose parents are unknown or undocumented, is called a "grade" horse. A grade horse is basically the equivalent of a mixed-breed dog in the dog world. But just like most mixed breeds are awesome dogs, grade horses can be great riding and companion horses for people.

Are any crossbred horses in breed registries?

Various horse breed organizations keep records, called breed registries or studbooks, of certain horse breeds. Some breed organizations will enter a crossbred horse into their registries as long as one of the horse's parents belongs to the breed the group represents (although sometimes they specify what the other parent must be). For instance, a paint horse must have one quarter horse parent, but the other parent can be any breed. A quarter horse can have one Thoroughbred parent and still be considered a quarter horse. An Appaloosa can have one Arabian, quarter horse, or Thoroughbred parent. Some registries specifically represent certain crossbreeds, like Aztecas (an Andalusian and quarter horse mix) and Morabs (a Morgan and Arabian mix).

What is the horse's poll?

The poll is the area between the horse's ears, at the top of the head near the beginning of the neck.

What is the muzzle?

The muzzle is the area at the end of a horse's face where its lips and nostrils are located.

What is a horse's dock?

The dock is the area at the back of a horse where its tail begins.

What is a horse's croup?

The croup is the area on a horse's back from the top of its hips to the dock of its tail.

What are a horse's fetlocks?

The fetlocks are the ankles of a horse.

What are the pasterns on a horse?

The pastern is the area between a horse's fetlock (ankle) and its hoof on each leg.

What are a horse's hocks?

The hocks are the knee joints on a horse's back legs. Unlike the horse's front knees, or our knees, the hocks bend backward, kind of like a human elbow.

Where are a horse's elbows?

Unlike our elbows, which are the arm joints halfway between our shoulders and wrists, a horse's elbows are at the top and back of its front legs, right underneath the bottom of its shoulders.

What is the hard area on the inward-facing side of a horse's knees and hocks (back knee joints) called?

Horses have small, hard growths on the inward-facing sides of each of their legs, a little above the knees on the front legs and a little below the hocks on the back legs. These hard patches are called chestnuts. Scientists think they may be the remains of extra toes that horses lost during their evolution. In horse lingo, you also hear the word chestnut to describe the coat colorings of some horses. Chestnut horses are various shades of red.

What are ergots?

Ergots are horn-like growths at the pointed part in the back of some horse's fetlocks (ankles). If a horse has them, they can be trimmed. Like chestnuts, they may be the remains of extra toes that horses lost during evolution.

What is the coronet?

The coronet, also called the coronary band, is the area of a horse's foot where the hairline stops and the hoof starts. The hoof material grows downward from the coronet.

What is the forelock?

The forelock is the hair that hangs from between a horse's ears onto its forehead. Think of it as a horse's bangs.

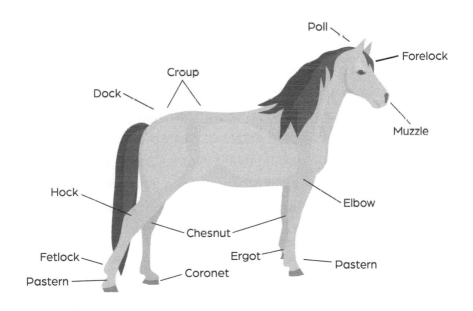

What is a general name for the gear used for riding and caring for horses?

Besides the horse itself, you need equipment to properly walk, ride on, or take care of a horse. Much of this equipment is strapped right to the horse. This equipment might include a saddle, stirrups, a bridle, reins, a bit, a lead, or a halter, among other things. The term for this collective equipment is tack, or horse tack. You might hear someone say "tacking up" to refer to strapping all the necessary equipment onto a horse to prepare to ride it. Taking all this equipment off after a ride is called "untacking." For more on types of tack, see chapter 4, "Take the Reins: Horse Training and Riding," on page 57.

What are the two major riding styles?

The two categories of riding styles you will hear about most are English riding and Western riding. English riding styles and tack developed from the historical needs of soldiers on horseback (and later also fox hunters) in England and parts of Europe. Western riding styles and tack developed from the needs of working cowboys in the Americas. English riding is common all over the world, not just in England. Western is most common in the US, but it can also be found in other countries. Both the Western and English styles are featured in different sports and show-riding events. You can learn more about these in chapter 6, "The Inside Track: Horses in Sports and Show."

In addition, there are riding styles that are subtypes of the two main styles. And there are other styles in various parts of the world that aren't practiced as widely, like Peruvian (a distinct riding style with unique tack practiced mainly in Peru).

What are the different horse gaits?

Gaits are the ways any animal with legs uses its legs to move from place to place. In the case of horses, gait categories include both speed and the way they place their feet on the ground as they move forward. There are many types of gaits, but here are the four basic horse gaits you'll hear about most, in order of speed:

- **Walk:** Much like a human, the horse puts one foot on the ground at a time during this slowest gait. But unlike a human, the horse has four feet, so the horse's walk has four beats.

- **Trot:** Faster than a walk, a trot is when two of the horse's feet hit the ground at the same time; the front foot on one side of the horse's body and the back foot on the opposite side hit on one step, and then the other front and back foot hit on the second step. This gives each step two beats.

- **Canter:** In the next fastest horse movement, one of the horse's back feet hits the ground, then the other back foot and one front foot hit at the same time, and then the final front foot hits, which gives the movement three beats.

- **Gallop:** A gallop is the fastest horse gait. During a gallop, all four feet are sometimes off the ground for a short time. One back foot hits the ground, then the other, then one front foot, and then the other. But it all happens very fast, making it four beats very close together.

There are other gait categories in the different riding styles or in some cases for the breed of the horse. For instance, the Western riding style also has a jog (somewhere between a walk and a trot) and a lope (somewhere between a trot and a canter). An unwanted horse behavior called "jigging" is a gait faster than a walk that a horse being ridden might do if it's anxious to get home. And certain so-called gaited horses have their own special gaits, like the Icelandic horse that has a gait called a *tölt*. You can read more about that in chapter 2, "It's Not Rocket Science: Horse Science and Biology," on page 43.

What is a gaited horse?

Members of a gaited horse breed have a smooth, distinctive gait that is unique to the breed. They tend to have a gait in which one foot is always on the ground, although they can gallop like other horses if needed. They are known for endurance and for being smooth rides, which makes them good for beginners. Some gaited horse breeds are the American saddlebred, American standardbred, Appaloosa, Kentucky Mountain saddle horse, Icelandic, Missouri fox-trotting horse, Paso Fino, Peruvian Paso, Rocky Mountain horse, and Tennessee walking horse.

What is a dorsal stripe on a horse?

Not every horse has this, but some horses have a dark stripe down their backs called a dorsal stripe. Some breeds known to often have dorsal stripes are the Argentine criollo, the Norwegian Fjord, and the Konik pony (a breed from Poland).

What are the terms for the various colors and patterns of horses?

Although all horses are unique, there are standard terms to categorize horse coloring and coat patterns. These terms can be based on the color of the horse's coat, the skin underneath the coat, mane and tail hair coloring, or sometimes patterns (like spots or stripes). Many horses also have white markings on their faces or lower legs that are not covered in these terms. Check out the next two entries for more on face and leg markings. Here are some common horse color or pattern (or both) descriptions:

- ♘ **Bay:** Medium brown coat with black tail and mane hair and black markings on the legs

- ♘ **Bay roan:** Bay coat with white hairs mixed throughout the coat

- ♘ **Black:** Completely black coat, tail, and mane

- ♘ **Blanket:** White coat (and possibly spots) draped over the back top of the horse starting just before the hips and going to the rear of the horse

- ♘ **Blue roan:** Black or very dark brown coat with white hairs mixed throughout

- ♘ **Brindle:** Striped pattern in the coat but more scattered and uneven than zebra stripes

- ♘ **Brown:** Very dark brown coat with a black tail and mane

- ♘ **Buckskin:** Golden or yellow coat with a black tail and mane

- ♘ **Chestnut:** Light to dark red coat, mane, and tail coloring (like the hair of a human redhead); also called sorrel

- ♘ **Dapple:** A gray horse with rings of darker hair around patches of lighter hair that form light spots all over

- ♘ **Dun:** A beige or reddish-brown horse, with darker muzzle, mane, leg, and tail coloring, often with a dark dorsal stripe down its back and sometimes leg stripes

- ♘ **Gray:** Despite the name, either a white or gray coat, but in either case, with darker skin; they also might be born a different color and go gray within a few years

- **Grulla:** Smoky dun with a black tail, mane, and leg coloring, and sometimes stripes
- **Leopard:** Light coat with dark spots like a leopard or dalmatian; also called Appaloosa, although Appaloosa is a breed with this pattern as well
- **Palomino:** Golden or yellow with a white tail and mane
- **Pinto:** Large patches of white and another color all over; in the British Isles, also called piebald (for white and black) or skewbald (for white and brown)
- **Red roan:** Chestnut coat with white hair mixed through-out
- **Snowflake:** Dark body with white spots
- **Strawberry roan:** Chestnut coat with white hair mixed throughout
- **White:** White coat and pink skin

What are the names for common horse facial patterns?

Each horse has distinctive face markings, but there are some common face-coloring patterns, each involving white or light-colored patches on the face. These patterns include the following:

- **Snip:** A small white strip between the nostrils
- **Star:** A patch of white between the eyes, often shaped a little like a four-sided star
- **Stripe:** A narrow strip of white from around the eyes down to the nostrils
- **Blaze:** A wide strip of white from the top of the face down to the mouth

- **White face:** White all over the face, also called a bald face

What are white patches above a horse's feet called?

Horse facial markings aren't the only ones with cute names. Horses often also have white markings above their hooves. If they have white patches that extend from their hooves to someplace near their fetlocks (ankles), these markings are called socks because it kind of looks like the horse is wearing socks. Likewise, if the white markings go up to near the hocks (knee joints) or above, they are called stockings.

What is a pinto horse?

Pinto is not a breed of horse but a color pattern on a horse. A pinto-type horse has large alternating patches of light and dark all over. Many breeds can be pintos. A paint horse is one breed that typically (but not always) has a pinto pattern. The three categories of pinto color patterns are as follows:

- **Tobiano:** White patches on the body, including across the top, and white legs
- **Overo:** White patches on the belly, neck, head, and legs but not across the top
- **Tovero:** Mostly white except the neck, poll (between the ears), and ears, and sometimes with blue eyes

What are the names for the sounds horses make?

Horses make four main sounds:

- **Neigh:** Also sometimes called a whinny, this loud, high-pitched, voiced sound is a social call meant to call out to other horses (or sometimes people), for instance, when a horse is separated from its herd.

⋃ **Nicker:** This is a soft, vibrating sound, almost like a purr. It is meant as a greeting, a request for food, a call from a mare to a foal to come back, or a call from a stud (a male horse for breeding) to a mare to attract the attention of a potential mate.

⋃ **Snort:** This is a loud and sudden expulsion of breath through the nostrils that usually means the horse is startled or feels threatened, although sometimes horses also snort playfully.

⋃ **Squeal:** This is a long, high-pitched cry meant as a sign of aggression or a show of dominance, usually toward another horse. (Horses may do a shorter and high-er-pitched squeal of fright though.) Watch out for flying hooves if you hear a horse squeal!

What is a draft horse?

Draft refers to breeds of horses originally bred to pull plows, carts, carriages, and other similar tools or vehicles. Because of their intended use, they are usually very large, muscular, and strong, with shorter legs than a lot of other breeds have.

What do heavy and light mean in horse lingo?

There are many ways to categorize horse breeds, and one is heavy versus light. Heavy horses, also called draft horses, are large, stocky, strong horses that are usually calm and gentle and were first used for things like hauling heavy loads, pulling plows, and carrying armored soldiers into battle (sometimes wearing armor of their own). Light horses tend to be thinner, smaller and more energetic, and were bred for riding and racing, among other purposes. Of course, heavy and light horses (and ponies) have been bred together, combining a large variety of traits and producing many breeds.

What is feathering on a horse?

No, horses don't have feathers. But some of them do have what is called feathering. This is long hair on the lower part of the legs that sometimes puffs out around the hooves. Horses with noticeable feathering tend to be heavy horses and ponies from cold climates, like the Clydesdale, Poitevin, shire, and Highland pony.

What does mounting a horse mean?

Mounting a horse just means the rider is getting onto a horse. Getting off the horse is referred to as dismounting.

What is a fenced outdoor horse enclosure called?

There are two types of outdoor horse enclosures. A large outdoor enclosure that includes enough grass for grazing is known as a pasture. A smaller fenced area that doesn't have much (or sometimes any) grass is called a paddock (also called a corral). In either case, a pasture or paddock should have some sort of shed structure that horses can shelter in during bad weather.

What is a run-in shed?

A run-in shed is a structure with a roof, three walls, and one open side that horses can run (or walk) into to seek shelter from the sun, rain, snow, wind, or other weather conditions. They are often found in paddocks and pastures where horses are kept.

What is a pipe corral?

A corral is a pen (fenced area) in which to keep horses or other livestock. A pipe corral is just what it sounds like—a corral with a fence made of pipes.

What is the name for an indoor horse enclosure?

Some horses are kept in stables, sometimes called box stables, which are indoor enclosures (four walls and a roof) for housing horses. One of the walls in an individual horse's box stable is often a half-height door so the horse can look out. Stables for more than one horse are large buildings with a box enclosure for each horse. Horses that live in stables still need to be let out into paddocks or pastures or taken out for walks or rides to keep them healthy and happy.

What is the name for an enclosed trailer used to transport horses?

A horse box is an enclosed trailer used to carry horses to other locations. People sometimes call them horse trailers. You may have seen a horse box being hauled by a truck or car on the road at some point. But that's not the only way to transport a horse. Horses are now also carried in special containers on planes!

What is a furlong?

A furlong is a way to measure distance. One furlong equals ⅛ of a mile, or about 660 feet. The furlong has been used to measure distance since ancient times, but today it is used most often in horse racing.

What is bucking?

Bucking is a movement a horse might do if it wants to throw something (like its rider) off its back. When a horse bucks, it jumps into the air with its back arched and its head down.

What is rearing up?

When a horse rears, or rears up, it stands on its back legs and lifts its front legs off the ground. Horses might rear up if something scares them or if part of their tack is hurting them.

What are "trekking" and "hacking" in reference to horse riding?

Trekking is riding a horse or pony on a long, usually slow trail ride, sometimes for hours and often in a group that forms a line of trekkers. Hacking is taking a horse out for a ride for exercise or leisure, and can be done solo or in a group. They are both usually activities that involve riding horses through the scenic countryside.

What is equinophobia?

Many people have a love of horses, but some people are frightened of them. One of the terms for an excessive fear of horses (or horse relatives like donkeys or mules) is equinophobia. It comes from *equus*, the Latin word for "horse," and *phobos*, the Greek word for "fear." The word hippophobia, which sounds like it would mean a fear of hippos, is actually another word that means a fear of horses. *Hippo* is the Greek word for "horse."

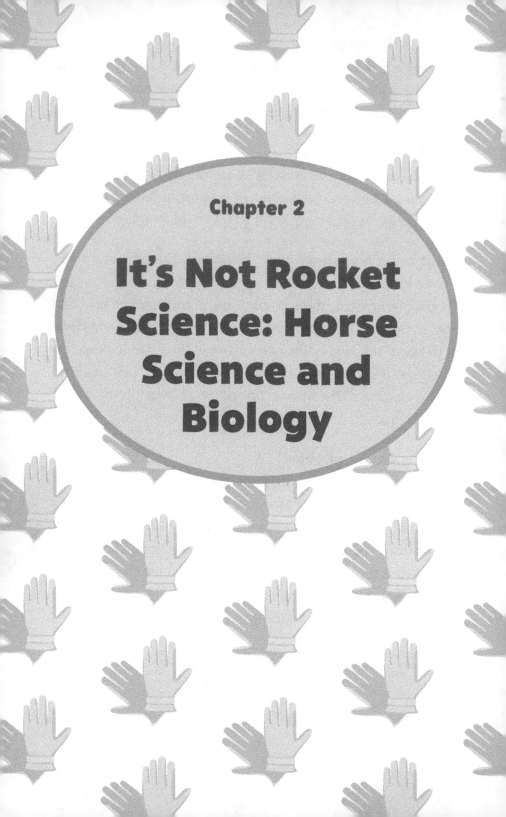

Chapter 2

It's Not Rocket Science: Horse Science and Biology

What is the scientific name for a horse?

The scientific name for a horse is *Equus ferus caballus*. One of the ways biologists (those who study living things) classify all life is by sorting it into these groups: kingdom, phylum, class, order, family, genus, and species (and sometimes subspecies). Each of these categories gets a name in Latin. Horses, along with people and all other animals, belong to the kingdom Animalia. Under the kingdom, each group includes a smaller and smaller number of related animals. For the modern domestic horse, these are the names for each of the categories:

- **Kingdom:** Animalia
- **Phylum:** Chordata
- **Class:** Mammalia
- **Order:** Perissodactyla
- **Family:** Equidae
- **Genus:** *Equus*
- **Species:** *E. ferus*
- **Subspecies:** *E. f. caballus*

What is an equine?

Equines are all the animals in the scientific genus *Equus*. That includes horses and some other horse-like animals. Over 60 species in the group are now extinct (no longer existing), but a few besides horses are still around today.

What nonhorse equines exist today?

Aside from domestic and wild horses, the other members of the genus *Equus* are two species of donkeys (*Equus asinus* and *Equus hemionus*) and three species of zebras (*Equus burchelli*, *Equus grevyi*, and *Equus zebra*).

What is the difference between a wild horse and a feral horse?

The term "wild horses" often refers to the undomesticated horses that roam free all over the world. But most of these free-roaming horses are really feral horses; this means they are the descendants of domesticated horses who were let loose or escaped from their owners rather than wild horses who don't have any domesticated ancestors. Only one species of truly wild horse exists on the planet today.

What species of wild horse exists today?

The only truly wild species of horse on the planet that we know of is Przewalski's (pronounced *shuh-val-ski*) horse. It was named for Russian explorer, geographer, and soldier Nikolai Przewalski, who presented a skull and hide to a museum that turned out to be from a wild horse.

Its scientific name is *Equus ferus przewalskii*, although some scientists believe it is really just a variety of *Equus ferus caballus*. But Przewalski's horse has slightly different genes from other modern horses—the genes in cells carry information that partly control the traits of living things. These horses are stockier and shorter than most domestic horses, closer to the height of the breeds we call ponies. A common ancestor of modern domestic horses and Przewalski's horses is thought to have split off into the two species around 500,000 years ago.

By the 1960s, Przewalski's horses were extinct (no longer existing) in the wild. The only ones left were held and bred in captivity. In the 1990s, groups of the equines were released back into their former natural habitats in Mongolia, China, and Kazakhstan. In Mongolia, they are called *takhi*, meaning "spirit." There are around 2,000 in the wild today. The largest group lives in

Hustai National Park in Mongolia. They are now considered an endangered species rather than extinct (no longer existing).

What is a mustang?

Mustangs are feral horses in the Americas that are descendants of horses brought over by the Spanish in the 1600s. The word mustang comes from the Spanish word for stray horse. Several varieties of mustangs run wild in the US today. They include the following breeds:

- ∪ Cerbat mustang
- ∪ Chincoteague pony
- ∪ Colonial Spanish horse
- ∪ Kiger mustang
- ∪ Pryor Mountain mustang
- ∪ Spanish mustang

What breed of mustang may have descended from horses who survived a shipwreck off the coast of a US island?

No one knows for sure how Chincoteague ponies got to Assateague Island, but they may be descended from horses who survived the shipwreck of a Spanish galleon hundreds of years ago. These feral ponies are short and stocky, standing about 12 to 13 hands high. Their bellies look more bloated than most horses because of their peculiar diet. They feed on cordgrass in salt marshes, so they eat a lot of salt and then drink about twice as much water as typical horses.

Half of the island is part of Maryland and half is part of Virginia. The Maryland-side ponies are taken care of by the National Park Service, and the Virginia-side ponies are taken care of by the Chincoteague Volunteer Fire Company. Every year the fire company holds an event called the Pony Swim, during which they herd the Virginia ponies in a swim from Assateague Island to Chincoteague Island, auction off some of the foals to raise money and keep the herd from getting too large, and swim them back the next day. People can visit the beaches of the islands and see the ponies in person, although visitors are warned not to get too close for safety's sake. Marguerite Henry released a popular children's novel in 1947 called *Misty of Chincoteague* about kids raising one of the ponies.

What breed of feral horse roams southern France?

The Camargue horse, also called "the horse of the sea," is a breed of feral horse that lives in the Rhône delta area in southern France. They are stocky horses with wide hooves who evolved inhabiting the harsh wetlands of the area. Camargue are usually born with dark coats that turn light gray as they age. Herds of them are protected in the Camargue Regional Park preserve. Some have been bred with other horses over the years, and domesticated Camargue are ridden by local cowboys as well as in dressage, racing, and other horse-riding events.

What body part of a horse is the largest of any land animal?

A horse's eyes are the largest of any land mammal, even the elephant! Horse eyes are about eight times larger than human eyes. Large eyes usually mean better vision. A scientific study found that animals that run faster are likely to have evolved larger eyes. And horses are known for speed. Horses, with their large eyes on the sides of their heads, can see almost 360 degrees (or in a full circle) around them. Imagine not having to turn your head to see the things all around you! But that "almost" means there are exceptions, which you can learn about next.

What are a horse's blind spots?

Horses have nearly 360-degree vision, but they have two blind spots: directly behind them and directly in front of them. That's one reason not to stand directly in front of or behind a horse. You might get a strong kick for standing behind a horse, and horse kicks can be deadly! The safe way to approach a horse is from the side.

How many eyelids does a horse have for each eye?

Each of a horse's large eyes has three eyelids, one at the top and bottom like ours and one underneath that moves diagonally.

How fast can horses go?

Most horses can gallop at nearly 40 miles per hour. You can learn about a breed that can run even faster in certain conditions later in this chapter on page 40. For comparison, the fastest human so far is Usain Bolt, who hit 27.5 miles per hour in his fastest race.

What is an ungulate?

Horses are odd-toed ungulates. An ungulate is any mammal that has hooves. The hooves are hard skin tissue covering wide toes. Odd-toed ungulates have an odd number of toes on their feet.

What other animals are closely related to equines?

Horses and their equine cousins are also related to rhinoceroses and tapirs. While rhinos and tapirs are not equines, all three animals belong to the scientific order Perissodactyla. All are odd-toed ungulates that originated in North America. Imagine rhinos roaming the US! Horses, rhinos, and tapirs are thought to share a common ancestor who likely originated in India.

What exactly is a horse's hoof compared to a human foot?

Each of a horse's hooves is a single toe covered in hardened skin tissue called keratin, which fingernails, toenails, and horns are made of—but also hair and feathers! The hard outer portion of the hoof is called the hoof wall, and it's made of hard, dead cells. This is why nailing horseshoes to this area of the hoof doesn't hurt horses. Since each hoof is one toe, and one is an odd number, horses are called odd-toed ungulates.

What part of a horse is called the frog?

The frog is a cushiony triangular pad inside of and protected by the hoof wall. Part of it is exposed and can be seen on the bottom of the hoof. It cushions the rest of the horse from the impact of its hooves on the ground. Since the frog is not hard like most of the hoof's exposed material, care needs to be taken not to poke the frogs when cleaning a horse's hooves. For more on caring for horses, see chapter 3, "Eat like a Horse: Feeding and Care."

How fast do horse's hooves grow?

Like our fingernails and toenails, a horse's hoof material grows continuously and either wears off or has to be trimmed. Growth rate varies from horse to horse and tends to get slower as horses age, but horse hooves grow back at an average rate of ¼ to ⅜ of an inch per month. That's like growing the equivalent of a whole new hoof every year!

How long does a foal develop inside its mother before being born?

A foal takes nearly a year to develop in the mare's womb before birth, while humans take around nine months to develop before birth.

How long does it take for a foal to stand up on its own?

Human babies begin to stand on their own from around 9 to 12 months old, but foals can do so about an hour after they are born!

What are "fairy slippers" on a horse?

Fairy slippers is one of the names for soft, rubbery tissue that covers a foal's hooves in the womb and at birth. This is also sometimes called fairy fingers, golden fingers, foal slippers, gills, or leaves, among other things. The technical name for this is the eponychium. This tissue protects the inside of the mother's womb and birth canal from the baby's hooves during pregnancy and birth. The eponychium on each of a foal's hooves begins to dry out just after the foal is born, and it wears away quickly as the foal stands and walks. It is usually mostly gone in a day. Human babies also have eponychium partially covering their fingernails and toenails in the womb. It also wears away, and all that's left is our cuticles.

When do horses reach adulthood?
Horses are fully grown at around four years of age.

How much does a horse's brain weigh?
On average, a human adult's brain weighs around 3 pounds. A horse's brain averages only 2 to 2½ pounds though, about the size of a human child's brain—even though most horses are much more massive than a person. But the ratio of brain size to body mass isn't the only thing that determines intelligence. Horses are smart creatures who are thought to have the intelligence level of a 12-year-old person. They can be trained to do many things, from responding to vocal commands to doing tricks, and horses have been known to memorize routes they take. One horse could apparently even count and spell! You can read about him in chapter 7, "The Horse and Buggy Days: History of the Horse," on page 103.

What body part of a horse takes up more room in its head than its brains?
A horse's teeth occupy more room in its head than its brain. Chew on that fun fact!

How many teeth does an adult horse have?
The answer to this is different by gender. An adult female horse typically has 36 teeth, while an adult male horse usually has a whopping 40 teeth. The four extra teeth in the males are canines, sometimes called fighting teeth. Some mares do have canines, but they are usually less developed than in males. Canines serve little purpose for the males since the upper and lower canines

do not touch. Often when a horse has sharp canines, the owner will have them filed down to protect others and the horse itself (a procedure known as floating a horse's teeth).

Can horses breathe through their mouths?

Astonishingly, the answer is no. Like us, horses can breathe through their noses, but unlike us, they can't breathe through their mouths. They breathe in and snort (exhale forcefully) through their noses once with each stride while running, and they hold their breath when jumping. Some competitive horse riders put adhesive nasal strips on their horse's nostrils during competitions to keep the horse's airways more open.

Can horses grab things with their lips?

Horses have prehensile lips, which means they can use them to grasp items.

How good is a horse's sense of smell?

A horse's sense of smell is thousands of times stronger than our sense of smell. They use this keen ability to check for nearby predators, among many other things.

How much saliva does a horse produce daily?

Humans produce only 2 to 4 pints of saliva daily. Four pints is only ½ of a gallon. But horses make around 10 gallons of saliva every day. That's a lot of spit!

Are horses ruminants like cows?

Horses are not ruminants. Ruminants are herbivores (eat only plants) and hoofed like horses. But unlike horses, they are two-toed (with split hooves), and they have a special way of digesting grasses and other plants. They lack the enzymes (types of proteins) to digest plants directly, so their stomachs are divided into four chambers. The plant matter they eat sits in the first chamber and begins to break down. Then the ruminants regurgitate the broken-down cud into their mouths—which is sort of like throwing up, but less violent—and chew it again. Next time they swallow, it goes to one of the other stomach chambers to complete digestion. Ruminants include cows, deer, giraffes, goats, and sheep, to name a few. But horses are not among them. They can digest plants directly in their one-chambered stomach. All ruminants have to do one thing that horses cannot. See the next entry for more.

Can horses throw up?

Horses can do many things, but vomiting isn't one of them. Horses have a band of muscles at the bottom of their throat where it meets the stomach (like a valve that opens to let food in and closes to keep it there). It is so strong that it keeps food from escaping back the other way. This part of the horse also enters the stomach at a lower point than it does for us, which makes it even harder for food to get pushed back up. Pressure makes it close tighter. And they don't have strong vomit reflexes like we do. Therefore, horses (for the most part) cannot throw up. If they do, something has gone very wrong inside.

This lack of vomiting ability is one reason digestive issues in a horse need to be treated immediately. They can lead to a potentially deadly illness called colic. You can learn more about this in chapter 3, "Eat like a Horse: Feeding and Care," on page 52. Fun fact: Horses aren't the only mammals that can't throw up. Most rodents, including mice and rabbits, can't either.

How many ear muscles does a horse have?

Horses have 10 muscles in each ear. For comparison, humans have only three muscles in each ear. Because of the extra muscles, horses can pivot their ears from front to back to better hear things around them. When horses are walking in a herd, the horses in the lead, in the middle, and in the rear will tilt their ears in different directions from one another to more efficiently detect predators.

How big is a horse's heart?

An average horse's heart weighs around 9 or 10 pounds and is about the size of a basketball. A human heart weighs from ½ of a pound to a little less than a pound and is somewhere between the size of a baseball and a softball.

How much sleep do horses need?

Humans need around eight hours of sleep per night to stay healthy, but horses need only up to three hours per night, which they can do either lying down or standing up.

How long do horses live?

Domestic horses live an average of 25 to 30 years. Smaller horses tend to last longer than larger horses (like dogs). Feral horses tend to have a shorter lifespan because of the harsh living conditions and lack of veterinary care. Learn about an astounding exception in the next entry.

What horse is known to have lived the longest?

Despite the average lifespan of the typical horse being much shorter than this, a barge-pulling draft horse in England lived from 1760 to 1822—a whopping 62 years!

In what era of earth's history did the earliest known ancestors of horses live?

The ancestor of the modern horse, called *Hyracotherium*, likely appeared during the Eocene epoch, which lasted from around 56 to 34 million years ago.

Where did horses come from originally?

The modern horse's ancestor, *Hyracotherium*, came from North America. Their descendants made their way to Europe and Asia across the Bering land bridge, which was frozen over during the last major Ice Age between 120,000 and 11,500 years ago. This is why horses could be found over most of the world even before they were domesticated. Unfrozen now, the former Bering land bridge is currently a body of water called the Bering Strait. Wild horses actually became extinct (no longer existing) in North America, but European colonists brought them back to the continent in the 14th century, and now there are many horses (feral and domesticated) there once again.

What was the dawn horse?

Another commonly used name for the horse ancestor *Hyracotherium* is *Eohippus*, the Greek roots of which mean "dawn horse." So dawn horse is another name for this original horse ancestor. The best preserved fossils of the dawn horse were found in the Messel Pit in Messel, Germany. The Messel Pit was a shale oil extraction site, but many well-preserved fossils, some with their body tissue intact, were found in the area. Because of this, it was named a World Heritage site by the United Nations Educational, Scientific, and Cultural Organization to protect it so scientific research can continue. The dawn horse samples are held in nearby museums, including one museum in the town of Messel close to the pit. Fun fact: Unlike most horses today, this horse ancestor was the size of a small dog.

What ancient equine is also known as the "American zebra"?

Equus simplicidens roamed the ancient Americas around 3.7 million years ago during the Middle Pliocene era. *E. simplicidens* is one of the earliest *Equus* species. It is more closely related to modern zebras than modern horses and is therefore called the American zebra. The species is also called the Hagerman horse because a large group of its fossils were discovered in Hagerman, Idaho. Fun fact: It has been named the official state fossil of Idaho.

When were modern horses domesticated?

As far as we know, humans first domesticated modern horses during the Bronze Age around 4200 BCE—over 6,000 years ago! Current research shows that these horses likely came from the vast, treeless plains in southern Russia. Selective breeding for certain traits in that region gave us *Equus ferus caballus*, the subspecies that eventually overtook all others across the world.

How big can horses get?

The tallest-known horse was a shire breed called Sampson, born in 1846, who stood over 21.2 hands high (a little over 7 feet). Contrarily, the smallest horse stood just over 4 hands high (around 17 inches). Depending on size and type, the weight of horses can vary from under 200 pounds to over 2,700 pounds— that's 700 pounds over a ton!

Who was Big Jake?

A more recent tallest-known horse, according to Guinness World Records, was the aptly named Big Jake at Smokey Hollow Farm in Poynette, Wisconsin. He was a Belgian horse who stood 20 hands high. He was 20 years old when he passed away in 2021.

How many facial expressions can horses make?

According to recent research, horses can make over 17 different facial expressions. That's 10 fewer than humans can make, but three more than our close relatives the chimpanzees. These expressions may allow us to interpret the emotions that horses are feeling.

Can horses really sleep standing up?

Yes, horses are able to sleep standing up. Their legs lock into place so they won't fall over. But they can also sleep lying down. And if they want to reach REM sleep (the "rapid eye movement" phase of sleep during which dreams occur), they can do so only while lying down. People do not have locking legs, so don't try this at home!

What gender is the typical leader of a horse herd?

An adult female horse usually heads each group of horses. When moving from place to place, the top mare takes the lead while the top male horse brings up the rear and the other herd members walk in between them.

How many modern horse breeds are there?

There are around 350 different breeds of horses today. They are grouped into several major types: draft horses; gaited horses; light horses; ponies; and hot-, cold-, or warmbloods.

Horses are put into breed categories based on their ancestors and certain shared traits.

What do the hotblood, coldblood, and warmblood categories mean?

These categories refer to the personalities and energy levels of horses and the climates in which they were originally bred. Hotbloods are fast and energetic and typically from warm climates. Coldbloods are the calmest horses. They are usually large, heavy breeds from cold places. Warmbloods are athletic but calmer than hotbloods. They possess a balanced combination of traits and come from breeding hotbloods and coldbloods together.

What three ancient horse types do all modern horse breeds come from?

All modern horses are descendants of three species of wild horses, only one of which still exists today:

- Forest horses (*Equus caballus silvaticus*)
- Wild tarpans (*Equus caballus gmelini*)
- Asiatic wild horses (*Equus przewalski* or *Equus caballus przewalski*), which are still around

What is a mule?

Mules result from breeding male donkeys with female horses. Mules are often used as pack animals to carry loads of goods (much like their donkey relatives). They were first bred by Sumerians in ancient Mesopotamia (modern Turkey and Iraq) around 4,000 years ago. Typically mules cannot reproduce offspring of their own. But in 2007, a mule in Colbran, Colorado, named Kate, who was part of a large herd of mules, somehow became pregnant and birthed a foal. To quote *Jurassic Park*, "Life finds a way."

What equine does a horse and a zebra produce?

When a horse and zebra have a baby together, that baby is a zorse! Like mules, they usually can't have babies.

What three stallions do all modern Thoroughbreds come from?

Modern Thoroughbreds all descend from three stallions imported into England from 1689 to 1730: the Byerly Turk, the Darley Arabian, and the Godolphin Barb. Recent analysis of horses' genes (the genes in cells carry information that controls the traits of living things) passed down from male to male shows that 95 percent of all Thoroughbreds descended from just one horse on the male line: a British horse named Eclipse (because he was born during a solar eclipse on April 1, 1764). Eclipse was descended from the Darley Arabian. He passed away in 1789 of an illness called colic. You can learn more about this in chapter 3, "Eat like a Horse: Feeding and Care," on page 52. The female lines of Thoroughbreds and other modern breeds are much more diverse.

What famous miniature horse was owned by a winery?

In 1962, the Regina Winery in Etiwanda, California, bought a dozen Falabella (a miniature horse breed from Argentina) stallions and used them as promotional mascots. They attended events pulling a little carriage bearing the winery logo. They named one with a spotted Appaloosa coat Chianti, and he became a sort of celebrity. Most US Falabellas come from these winery stallions. You can learn more about this tiny breed on page 42.

What does the name Thoroughbred refer to?

The studbook (or official record) for English Thoroughbreds was closed in 1793; this means that only horses descended from very specific bloodlines that were registered before that time can be officially called Thoroughbreds. The term thorough-bred means the horses have been bred thoroughly, and there will be no more crossbreeding to introduce new traits. When non-Thoroughbred horses are bred with registered Thorough-bred stallions, their offspring are known as half-bred in Great Britain and Grade Thoroughbreds in the United States.

What fluffy Arctic horse breed hibernates while standing to survive the freezing cold?

The Yakut people likely migrated from Mongolia to Siberia sometime between the 1200s BCE and 1400s BCE, bringing their horses with them. These horses' descendants live farther north than any other horses on the planet. Temperatures in Yakutia sometimes reach as low as –70 degrees Fahrenheit. Over time, Yakutian horses adapted to withstand these extremely low temperatures. They are short and stocky; have long, thick hair; and have an ability that no other horse has called standing hibernation. This means their heart rate, breathing, and metab-olism slow down so they don't use much energy and don't need many nutrients. Fun fact: They are the only horses that hiber-nate, and they do it standing up!

What breed of horse was discovered by the US Bureau of Land Management in 1977?

During a roundup and relocation of horses in Beatty's Butte, Oregon, in 1977, someone from the US Bureau of Land Management noticed a bunch of horses with similar dun coloring and other common traits. After separating and studying them, their ancestry was traced back to the Iberian horses of Spanish colonizers, which were thought to have disappeared from the United States. Special herd management areas were set up for these feral horses, whose breed was named Kiger mustang.

What is the United States' most populous breed of horse?

The American quarter horse is one of the oldest US horse breeds, originating around the 1660s. They are also the most populous horses in the United States—and even worldwide! There are over four million quarter horses.

What ability is the American quarter horse named for?

The American quarter horse, sometimes just called a quarter horse, got its name because it can run races of a quarter mile or less faster than any other horse. Horses can run around 40 miles per hour on average, but American quarter horses have been clocked at an amazing 55 miles per hour!

What horse was first bred to carry kettledrums and their players for the English royals' Household Cavalry?

The drum horse is a breed of draft (or draught) horse originally bred in England to carry kettledrum players and their heavy 300-pound drums during processions that included the English royal family's Household Cavalry. Because the riders are playing drums with their hands, they control the reins with their feet. The breed was created to be large (over 16 hands high), strong, and gentle, and they usually came from crossbreeding horses like the Clydesdale, Irish Cob and shire. They are now kept by others, including nonroyals, for riding.

What is the world's biggest horse breed?

The shire horse, which originated in Great Britain, is the world's largest horse breed. It has huge hooves draped with long hair, can grow as much as 21.2 hands high (over 7 feet), and can pull loads of up to 5.5 tons in weight. This heavy horse is also known for its gentle personality.

Aside from dwarf ponies, what is considered the smallest pony breed?

The adorable Shetland pony originally hailed from the Shetland Islands off the coast of Scotland. They reach a maximum height of around 46 inches but average closer to 40 inches high, which makes them the smallest pony breed (there are smaller dwarf ponies, which are ponies that have gene changes that make them smaller than their breed normally is). Shetland ponies weigh up to 440 pounds, but are very strong for their size. Fun fact: the little critters are capable of hauling twice their weight! They are popular as children's riding ponies, although they also have a history of being used as pack animals. Shetlands are fluffy because of a double coat that keeps them warm in their native cold climate. Although considered the smallest pony breed, they are not the smallest horse breed. Read on to find out about a truly tiny horse!

What is the smallest breed of horse?

The smallest breed of horse is the Falabella, which stands only about 7.5 hands high (around 30 inches). These tiny horses are considered miniature horses and not ponies. They are tiny but have the body proportions of a larger horse. They were developed by crossbreeding small Argentinian horse breeds with other breeds over nearly 100 years. Patrick Newell started breeding these horses in 1845; his son-in-law, Juan Falabella, continued the work in 1879; and Julio Falabella formalized what is now known as the Falabella breed in the 1940s. Similar to how small dog breeds live longer than large dog breeds, Falabellas tend to live into their 40s, twice the lifespan of the average horse. Fun fact: Jackie Kennedy, the wife of former US president John F. Kennedy, had several Falabella horses. You can learn more about Falabellas in the earlier entry on page 38.

How long have New Forest Ponies been around?

The New Forest breed of pony has been around since around 1016 CE. They are from the New Forest area in southwest Hampshire in England, where untamed herds of these horses still roam and live among the locals. They've actually been there since before the area was named the New Forest.

What was the first documented horse breed from the United States?

The Morgan breed is named for Justin Morgan, a teacher in Vermont who was gifted a foal named Figure. Figure was born in 1789 and given to Morgan as a yearling (1 year old). Figure was used as a plow and logging horse and was known for being able to pull very heavy loads like a draft horse, but he could also beat Thoroughbreds in horse races. This made him a popular breeding horse. Figure was often called "Morgan's horse," which led to the breed name. Sadly, Figure died in 1821 after being injured when another horse kicked him, but the breed lived on in his children. The Morgan is thought to be the first-documented truly American breed. The all-purpose Morgan was once the most popular breed in the United States.

What spotted pony breed has striped hooves?

The pony of the Americas has both a spotted coat and striped hooves. The breed was first developed in the United States in the 1950s.

What pony breed is known for having one distinctive gait more than the usual four gait types?

The Icelandic horse is a pony breed from Iceland that reaches up to 14 hands high and 850 pounds and has a double coat to protect it from Iceland's cold temperatures. Rather than just walk, trot, canter, and gallop, it also does a fast walk called *tölt*.

What breed is named for its state of origin and its unique gait?

The Tennessee walking horse, or Tennessee walker, is named both for its state of origin and the unique running walk that is its usual gait.

What is the most popular draft horse in the United States?

A draft, or draught, horse pulls carts, plows, and other heavy items. The large Belgian breed—which, as you might guess, originated in Belgium—weighs up to 2,000 pounds and stands up to 17 hands high. It used to be very popular for heavy agricultural work and is currently the most popular breed for pulling heavy loads in the United States.

What heavy horse is known for its ability to walk on muddy ground?

Most heavy horses have feathered feet, which means they have long, thick fur covering their hooves. This makes it hard for them to walk in mud. But the Suffolk punch is a heavy horse that doesn't have the usual feathering around the feet, which makes them much less likely to get stuck in the mud. All Suffolk punch horses are descended from a single stallion who was born in Suffolk, England, in 1768. The Suffolk punch is the smallest of the heavy horse breeds.

What breed of horse was developed for working in vineyards?

The Breton, which originated in Brittany, a region in France, was first used to work in vineyards—places where people grow grapes and produce wine from them. The Breton breed is stocky and muscular with short legs.

Chapter 3

Eat like a Horse: Feeding and Care

What do horses eat?

Foals live for about their first year on their mother's milk before they graduate to the horse's typical diet. Horses are prey animals, not predators, meaning they don't hunt and kill other animals for their food (other animals hunt and kill them). Like most prey animals, horses are herbivores, which means they eat a plant-based diet.

They mainly eat grass or hay. Hay is either dried grass (of various possible types) or dried legume plants like clover or alfalfa. In addition, horses can occasionally be fed oats and other grains to supplement their diet and veggies and fruits like carrots and apples as treats. Hay bales, as well as commercial hay cubes and feed pellets, are available at feed and tack stores. A food called "hard feed" is grain mixed with vitamins that is often given to racehorses to give them extra energy. Horses also enjoy sugar cubes, but just like with people, too much sugar isn't good for them. After assessing a horse's health and diet, a vet may recommend supplements like vitamins, minerals, and fatty acids. One method of administering minerals is a mineral salt block for the horse to lick. See the next entry to learn about an exception to horses being strict herbivores.

What is the only horse breed known to hunt other animals?

Icelandic horses live on grasses just like other horses. But they have also been observed hunting and eating fish from the ocean! Unlike most other horses, this makes them omnivores.

Aside from being herbivores (mostly), what two other major traits of horses are due to their status as prey animals?

Horses use their amazing senses of sight, smell, and hearing to stay alert for danger because they are prey animals (those that other animals hunt and kill for food). And they have a couple of behavioral traits common to other nonpredators. These animals, as a rule, are always on the lookout for predators (animals that hunt and kill others for food) and other dangers. First, horses startle very easily. Unfamiliar things, loud noises, and sudden moves—including things like a car backfiring, a human opening an umbrella, a floating plastic bag, or a dog barking—can scare a horse and make it buck or flee, even with a rider on its back. Second, horses are herd animals. This means they form large groups called herds that stick together to provide safety in numbers against predators.

How many times a day should horses be fed?

Ideally, horses should be kept out most of the day in a grass-covered pasture where they can graze when they want, which they may do for up to 18 hours per day. If a pasture isn't available, horses should be fed at least twice a day, but more daily feedings are better to keep them healthy and happy. If a horse isn't prone to overeating, you can leave hay in front of it all day so it can eat when hungry. Horses evolved grazing at will, and frequent feedings keep their digestive systems working as they were meant to.

What type of grass can cause miscarriages in pregnant mares?

Typically horses can eat many different types of grass, including fescue. But fescue has been known to cause miscarriages (meaning the developing foal exits the womb before it can survive on its own) in pregnant mares.

How much food do horses need?

Although the exact amount varies by a horse's size, age, activity level, metabolism (the way cells produce energy), the climate it lives in (horses need more calories to keep warm in the cold), and other factors, horses generally need to eat about 1.5 to 3 percent of their body weight daily. For a horse that weighs 1,000 pounds, that's 15 to 30 pounds of food a day. Ideally, most of it should be roughage (food that's high in fiber, which is long, narrow, thick-walled plant cells that horses can digest but humans cannot) like grass or hay, although grains and supplements can be added for horses that need more nutrients. Commercial food cubes and pellets are also an option (they are mainly made of hay).

What unit of measurement is used to describe the portions hay bales are divided into?

When hay is baled, it is divided into layers that are easy to separate. Each one of these layers is called a "flake." While some recommend feeding a certain number of flakes daily, it is better to feed a horse by weight. So at least one flake per bale should be weighed to know how many flakes a horse needs daily.

What is forage?

When talking about horse feed, people sometimes use forage instead of hay.

What is an informal term for an overweight horse?

A horse who has become overweight is sometimes referred to as an "easy keeper." The term really means the horse needs less food to maintain its ideal body weight.

How much water do horses drink?

Like food, the amount of water needed varies from horse to horse. On average, though, horses drink about 8 to 14 gallons of water per day. For comparison, the recommended water intake for humans is about 8 cups of water a day, which is only ½ of a gallon. Horses need constant access to water.

Do horses drink water with their tongues like dogs?

Horses do not use their tongues to drink water like dogs (or cats). Instead, they suck the water into their mouths using their lips.

How much bedding should be kept in a horse's stable?

A horse's box stable should have at least 8 inches of bedding to make the horse comfortable when it lies down, protect its hooves and legs from the hard floor or ground underneath, and absorb urine. Bedding can be made of materials such as peat, sawdust, wood shavings, wood pellets, and straw. Only horse-safe materials should be used.

How often should a horse's stable be cleaned out?

Most humans these days have access to toilets and sewage systems to move their waste away from them, but there are no horse toilets. Horses pee and poop wherever they are when they need to go, and they produce a lot of urine and manure (poop) every day (from all that water and roughage—food high in fiber—they drink and eat). Horses enclosed in stables and paddocks rely on humans to clean up after them and get waste that might carry disease away from them. Stables should be cleaned every day to keep horses healthy, which includes removing manure and any urine-soaked bedding. But it's also a good idea to clean up manure piles in open fields, too, since they attract flies and breed bacteria and parasites that can infect and harm horses (and people). They also don't smell so great.

What tool is made for picking up horse manure?

A special tool called a manure fork is used to pick up horse manure. Unlike a shovel, it allows any dirt you pick up with the manure to fall through. Another handy thing you might want to have nearby when scooping manure is a wheelbarrow. The waste has to be hauled away somehow.

What does it mean to longe a horse?

Longeing is a way to both spend time with a horse and exercise it from the ground rather than while riding it. In longeing, a person puts a halter, longeing cavesson (an English-style type of noseband), or bridle on the horse's head; attaches a longe line to it (which is a 25- to 30-foot line, like a very long lead line or leash); and lets the horse walk around them in a big circle. The person might use verbal cues or something called a longe whip to instruct the horse to move. The whip is not used to beat the horse, thankfully, but rather to lightly tap it on the hocks (backside of the back legs) or to whip the ground as a cue.

How much exercise do horses need?

Horses evolved roaming free in grasslands. They even walk while they are eating. So naturally they need a lot of exercise and freedom to move. If a horse is in a confined space like a stable, it should be walked for 30 minutes a day, ridden for 45 minutes a day, or released into a larger open area to run around. Horses that don't get enough exercise can develop health problems, especially leg issues. Sometimes they can develop troubling behaviors called stable vices, which you can learn about in the next entry.

What are stable vices?

When a horse is subjected to the isolation of a box stable or small paddock for too long and doesn't get the exercise, socialization, or feeding frequency it needs, it can develop mental issues called stable vices. These behaviors include the following:

- **Bolting feed:** Eating way too fast, which can cause issues including a dangerous condition called colic (see the next entry for more information)
- **Cribbing or wind sucking:** Two similar behaviors, the first involving a horse placing its upper teeth on an object, arching its neck, and sucking air into its stomach, and the second involving the horse just sucking air into its stomach
- **Pacing:** Just as it sounds, continuously walking back and forth in its small enclosure
- **Weaving:** Shifting its weight from side to side, making its head move back and forth

All of these are signs a horse's needs aren't being met, and this should be remedied.

What is colic?

Colic is a dangerous, but common, condition in which a horse experiences severe digestive upset. Unfortunately, it can be deadly. Colic has many possible causes, including parasites, eating things it shouldn't (including moldy feed), eating too fast, going too long between feedings, not drinking enough water, exercising too soon before or after eating, vitamin or mineral deficiencies, too much time confined in a stable, food type or amount being changed suddenly, and a host of other things. In other words, a horse's digestive system is a sensitive one. The best course of action is prevention, and when signs of colic arise, a vet should be called immediately.

What does it mean to say a horse has gone lame?

A lot of people associate lameness with a horse having a limp. A limp can be a sign of lameness, but the actual definition of lameness is any change to a horse's gait. Such a change might mean the horse is having mobility issues and needs to see a vet immediately. Motion is very important for horses, and lameness can be a life or death situation.

Does a horse need to be put down if it breaks a leg?

In many Western films, when a horse breaks its leg, the owner shoots it to put it out of its misery. Horses used to be considered useless after a leg break because such breaks were hard to set and heal properly in such a way that the horse could continue living a healthy life. But these days, veterinarians have developed surgeries that can fix a broken leg and get the horse back on its feet, provided the owner can afford the expense. Just like our other furry companions, sometimes horses get euthanized (killed in a painless way) when they get terribly sick or injured. But unlike in the movies, it's with a humane medication rather than a firearm these days.

What does it mean when a horse is barn sour?

Barn-sour horses are hesitant to leave their barns or other homes for some reason. It could be that they just don't want to go because that's where they feel safe, but it could also be because they are in some sort of pain.

What is turnout?

Turning out a horse just means letting a horse go into a pen or pasture to run around on its own for a while. This is especially important for horses who are kept penned up in stables for long periods of time.

What basic grooming steps do horses need?

Horses need their coats to be brushed often (daily, if possible, but at least before and after rides), and occasionally also washed with water (preferably warm) and possibly shampoo. Grooming horses helps keep them free of dirt and debris that can irritate them when you put on tack. Their manes and tails also need to be brushed frequently to limit tangling, and washed and occasionally shampooed too. Their tails (and even their manes) can be braided to keep them neat and tangle-free, and their tails can be put into a special tail bag for protection.

A horse's hooves need to be cleared of dirt and debris, and they need to be trimmed at least every eight weeks. If a horse wears shoes, those need to be replaced just as often. The hooves need to be trimmed at a particular angle, so it's best to have a specialist handle trimming and reshoeing. See the next entry to learn more.

What specialist cares for a horse's hooves?

A horse's hooves are basically toenails, and, like toenails, they grow and need to be trimmed. Horses that are ridden or put to work also need their shoes replaced regularly. Shoes keep their hooves from cracking and splitting. The specialist who trims a horse's hooves and replaces its shoes is called a farrier.

What are some common horse-grooming tools?

Grooming horses requires many tools. Here are some of the most common (and essential):

- ♘ **Sponges:** Used to apply warm water to a horse's coat during occasional bathing

- ♘ **Cloths or towels:** Used to wipe down a horse after brushing or bathing and to clean its nostrils and other areas

- ♘ **Buckets:** Special bacteria–resistant buckets made for use with horses, along with a sponge and water, can be used for cleaning (and also for feeding and watering a horse)

- ♘ **Shedding blade:** A metal tool with a serrated (jagged like a saw) edge for removing loose hair a horse is shedding—used cautiously on its body and never on its legs

- ♘ **Shedding stone:** An alternative to the blade, this rough pumice stone is used for removing loose hair that's been shed

- ⋃ **Sweat scraper:** A tool for scraping liquid off a horse's coat, recommended for removing water from a horse after washing to help dry it off quickly rather than for scraping away sweat; some sweat scrapers also come with a toothy side that can double as a shedding blade
- ⋃ **Hoof pick:** A special pick for removing dirt and debris from the bottom of a horse's hooves
- ⋃ **Hoof brush:** A brush used to remove loose dirt from the outside and bottom of a horse's hoof
- ⋃ **Clippers:** Special electronic hair-removal devices for cutting off stray and overly long hair or trimming down horses' winter coats, usually with replaceable blades (scissors may also be used for this)
- ⋃ **Currycomb:** A comb (usually rubber or metal) used to loosen dirt and prep a horse for brushing (it can also clean dirt and debris out of other brushes used for grooming)
- ⋃ **Dandy brush (or stiff brush):** A brush with stiff bristles for brushing dirt out of a horse's coat
- ⋃ **Soft brush:** A brush with softer bristles to get the outer-most layer of dirt off and to groom sensitive areas like the face
- ⋃ **Mane and tail brush or comb:** A tool for brushing (or combing) a horse's mane and tail, which have much longer hair than a horse's coat hair

At what time of year do horses tend to shed?

Horses tend to shed their winter coat in the spring. This loose hair can be removed with a shedding stone, a shedding blade, or the jagged side of a metal currycomb.

Who (or in some cases what) walks a racehorse after a race or training?

When horses perform strenuous activity, one way for them to cool down is to go for a more leisurely walk (like people cooling down after a workout). Sometimes a person leads a horse on this walk, but there is also a machine that walks horses on leads around in a circle. The machine and the person are both called a "hot walker."

What is a bridle path?

A bridle path is an area that is sometimes shaved off a horse's mane behind its ears to keep the mane from getting caught and tangled in the bridle.

Chapter 4

Take the Reins: Horse Riding and Gear

What are reins?

Reins are leather straps that a horse rider holds onto and pulls (gently) in different directions to direct their horse where to go or to have the horse stop or back up. Reins are like the steering wheel, gear shift, and brake pedal in a car all in one! A rider's legs and vocal cues are also often used along with pulling the reins to control a horse.

What are split reins?

Some reins are one continuous strap with ends that attach on each side of the horse's bridle. But some riding styles (mainly Western) use split reins where each rein is a separate strap and the rider has to hold both.

What piece of equipment are the reins attached to?

The reins are attached to both sides of the bit, which is a piece of equipment, usually made of metal, in the horse's mouth.

What piece of horse gear is the bit attached to besides the reins?

The bit is attached to the headstall, a sort of strappy harness, or piece of gear, that goes around the horse's head. The head-stall, reins, and bit all make up the bridle. There is a bridle that doesn't require a bit called a hackamore bridle, which uses a noseband instead of a bit.

What two items of tack does a person use to lead a horse around from the ground?

When someone needs to stand on the ground and lead a horse somewhere, they use a halter and lead rope. The halter is a sort of harness (piece of equipment) composed of multiple straps that fit around the horse's head, plus a ring at the bottom for connecting the lead rope. The lead rope is a single long strap, much like a dog's leash, that a person uses to walk a horse. But you don't walk a horse exactly as you'd walk a dog. It's best to hold the lead close to the horse's halter and to stay to the horse's side (typically the left side) to prevent being trampled. And lead lines aren't just used for leading a horse. See the next entry for another use.

What is a hitching post?

A hitching post is a horizontal post or rail where you can tie your horse's lead line (usually attached to a halter on its head) so the horse doesn't wander off. You see them a lot in films set in the Old West, but they still exist in the horse world. Using a quick-release knot to tie up a horse is safest in case it panics and bolts. Someone might tie their horse to a hitching post while grooming them, although other methods for securing a horse exist.

What alternative to using a single line and a hitching post do many equestrians use?

Instead of a single lead line tied to a post, many equestrians use something called cross ties to secure their horses but also give them a little more sense of freedom. Cross ties are two lines attached to the horse's halter from opposite directions, usually attached to a wall. Like hitching posts, cross ties can keep a horse in one place when needed, for instance, while being groomed (or cleaned).

What part of a bridle wraps around the nose?

There are many different types of bridles, and they have different parts and pieces used for various riding styles, events, and purposes. Many bridles have a strap called the noseband that wraps around the lower part of the horse's muzzle near the nostrils.

What parts of a typical bridle wrap around the upper part of a horse's head?

A strap on a bridle that rests on the top of the horse's head from ear to ear is the browband. A strap that wraps underneath the horse's jaw near the throat is called the throatlatch. In fact, that area of a horse where its jaw meets its neck is called the throatlatch too.

What's the difference between a halter and a bridle?

Both are strappy harnesses, pieces of equipment that go around a horse's head, but they have different purposes. When a person is going riding in whatever style, the horse is fitted with a bridle, to which the reins and bit (unless it's a bit-less bridle) are attached. A halter is what a person straps to the horse's head when they want to lead the horse somewhere from the ground or secure them somewhere to keep them from running off or moving around. A halter has a ring to attach a lead (a leash-like strap for leading a horse around). A horse rider or caretaker will use a halter when walking or grooming a horse or doing any similar activity during which they don't want the horse to leave or buck.

What is neck reining?

There are different ways to direct a horse depending upon riding style and the horse's training, usually involving both the reins and the rider's legs. In neck reining, the rider pulls the reins in the direction they want the horse to turn so that the rein on the opposite side touches the horse's neck. This movement usually occurs in conjunction with pressure from the left leg if turning right and the right leg if turning left.

What gear sometimes attached to the bridle obstructs the horse's peripheral (or side) vision?

Some riders attach blinkers (or blinders) to their horse's bridle. These are little shields at the sides of the eyes to block the horse's rear and side vision. Blinkers help keep horses from getting distracted by things going on around them when they are being ridden, pulling carriages, or performing other activities where they need to be focused.

What is the name of the seat a rider puts on a horse?

Most riders strap a special seat called a saddle to their horse, although some people ride bareback without a saddle. Saddles usually look like they are made of leather, but it's really leather wrapped around a wood or fiberglass frame, kind of like an upholstered chair.

What is a latigo strap?

This is a strap on a Western saddle that holds the saddle on the horse.

What is a bucking strap?

This strap is tied around the haunches of a horse to make it buck. It is most commonly used to make horses buck in entertainment, for instance, in TV and movies, because bucking is not something people normally want a horse to do.

What are the subcategories of the English riding style?

Within the English riding style, there are three main types that have their own styles, rules, and saddles and other tack:

- ♘ **Hunt seat:** A popular style derived from fox hunting

- ♘ **Dressage:** An old and dance-like style derived from military cavalry movements (learn more in chapter 6, "The Inside Track: Horses in Sports and Show," on page 78)

- ♘ **Saddle seat:** A newer style described in more detail below

Which subcategory of English riding actually originated in the US?

Saddle-seat riding originated in the southern United States. A show saddle is used in saddle-seat riding. This saddle is flatter and has the rider sitting farther back from the withers (tops of the shoulders) than dressage and hunt-seat saddles. This frees up the horse's withers for better range of motion. The rider's legs are also more in front of them than underneath them as they are in the other English riding styles. Saddle seat also requires a double bridle, which has two sets of reins attached to two separate bits in the horse's mouth.

What are the two bits used in saddle-seat riding?

The saddle-seat rider's tack includes a double bridle with two sets of reins and two bits. These bits are the curb bit and the snaffle bit. The rider uses the reins attached to the curb bit to control the position of the horse's head and the reins attached to the snaffle bit to control how high the horse holds its head.

What is a Pelham bit?

A Pelham bit is a type of single bit to which two sets of reins can be attached. It is sort of like a snaffle bit and curb bit combined, but doesn't give the rider as much independent control of the reins as a double bridle with two separate bits.

On a saddled horse, where does the rider put their feet?

Stirrups hang from either side of the bottom of the saddle. Stirrups are loops with flat footrests at the bottom where the rider can rest their feet while riding. They are sometimes called stirrup irons (in English riding). Proper riding form calls for resting the balls of the feet in the stirrups.

How do Western and English stirrups differ?

English stirrups (sometimes called stirrup irons) tend to be made of metal, while Western stirrups are usually wood covered in leather. Western saddles come with stirrups already attached to them, while English saddles and stirrups come separately and have to be attached to the saddle by the rider or another horse caretaker.

What is the frame under the leather of a saddle called?

The wood or fiberglass frame underneath the leather is called a saddletree.

What are the three main parts of the top of a saddle?

The upper part of a saddle has three parts:

- **Pommel:** The part that sticks up at the front of the saddle

U **Seat:** The middle part that the rider sits on

U **Cantle:** The part that rises up at the back of the saddle

What are the different types of saddles?

There are several different types of saddles made for different types of riding and equestrian activities. Here are the main ones:

U Dressage saddle

U Endurance saddle

U Hunt-seat saddle

U Show saddle

U Western saddle

What piece of tack is used to secure the saddle to the horse?

A strap called a cinch in Western riding or a girth in English riding is secured around the horse's underside to keep the saddle on. Western saddles tend to come with cinches, but you usually have to purchase a girth separately for English-riding saddles. Cinches and girths can be made of leather or nonnatural materials. Girth covers can be bought and used to make the girth or cinch more comfortable for the horse.

What is riding a horse without a saddle called?

When someone rides a horse without a saddle, it's called bareback riding (or riding bareback). And since saddles didn't always exist, there was probably a lot of bareback riding in our history. Bareback can mean riding a horse with nothing between rider and horse, but there is an item of horse tack known as a bareback pad that can be secured around the horse to ride without the hard seat-like form of a saddle but with a bit of cushioning between rider and horse. Some bareback pads even come with stirrups.

What is a mounting block?

When a rider gets on a horse, it is usually referred to as mounting the horse. A mounting block is an aid to mounting a horse that is basically a small set of stairs with at least two steps for the rider to climb to make it easier to get into the saddle. A mounting block is commonly used with English riding, in which the stirrups usually hang higher on the saddle than Western saddle stirrups.

What piece of horse tack can be put beneath the saddle to make the horse more comfortable?

A saddle blanket or saddle pad, or sometimes saddlecloth in English riding, is placed between the saddle and the horse to act as a cushion for the horse's comfort.

What two pieces of horse tack keep the saddle from sliding forward or backward on the horse?

A breastplate is secured around the horse's chest to keep the saddle from sliding backward. A crupper is secured around the back of the horse under the tail to keep the saddle from sliding forward.

What sort of saddle was commonly used by women starting in medieval times?

In medieval times, from around 500 to 1500 CE, all the way through to the early 1900s, it was considered vulgar for a woman to sit with a leg over each side of a horse. A special sort of saddle called a sidesaddle was invented so that women could ride sitting sideways with both legs hanging over the same side of a horse.

What is a sidesaddle crop?

A sidesaddle crop is a stick-like tool that someone riding side-saddle can use to give their horse cues on the side opposite of where their legs are located. When riding astride (one leg on each side of the horse), a rider can move one leg or the other to signal the horse what to do. But sidesaddle riders have both legs on the same side of the horse (usually the left side), so they can use the crop to signal on the other side instead.

What are jodhpurs?

Jodhpurs are a style of pants that people who participate in traditional English-style riding frequently wear. They are quite narrow in the lower leg area to make them easy to wear with riding boots, which are sometimes referred to as jodhpur boots. Riding boots have heels that keep a rider's feet from slipping all the way through the stirrups, which it's good to prevent as it can lead to the rider being dragged by the horse.

What sort of head gear should a rider wear?

Horse riders often wear a hard helmet. This protects the rider's head if they fall (or are thrown) from a horse. It's similar to a bicycle helmet.

What gear prevents horses from being startled by loud or sudden noises?

The answer is simple: earplugs! Special horse-size earplugs exist and are sometimes used to keep horses from being startled by unexpected and loud noises. They are especially common for racehorses, which run past yelling spectators and other loud noises. They don't look quite like human earplugs. Horses have much larger and more cavernous ears than we do, so their earplugs are rounder and puffier.

How are horseshoes attached to the horse's feet?

Horseshoes are arch-shaped pieces made of metal or plastic that attach to the bottom of a horse's hooves to protect them from the hard ground. Horseshoes can be glued on or nailed on. But don't worry. The nails don't hurt the horse because of its hard and thick hoof material.

What piece of gear attached to the rider's shoe is used to prod the horse into movement?

Spurs are metal implements sometimes attached to the back of a rider's boots that are used to prod the horse into movement. It's the reason "to spur" can also mean to push or encourage someone to do something. English-style spurs just have a hard, blunt extension on the back of the boot. When most people think of spurs, they likely envision Western-style spurs that have a spinning, star-shaped wheel on the back called a rowel. Used incorrectly, spurs can hurt the horse.

In trail riding, what does it mean when you see a red ribbon tied to the base of a horse's tail?

Some horses don't behave well around other horses or sometimes around people either. When a rider has a red ribbon tied around the base of their horse's tail, it's a warning to other riders not to approach too close or their horse might kick out at the tailgating horse and rider.

What is the Pony Club?

The Pony Club is a worldwide association that specializes in teaching children horsemanship (how to ride and care for horses) through sport. And you don't have to own your own horse to join!

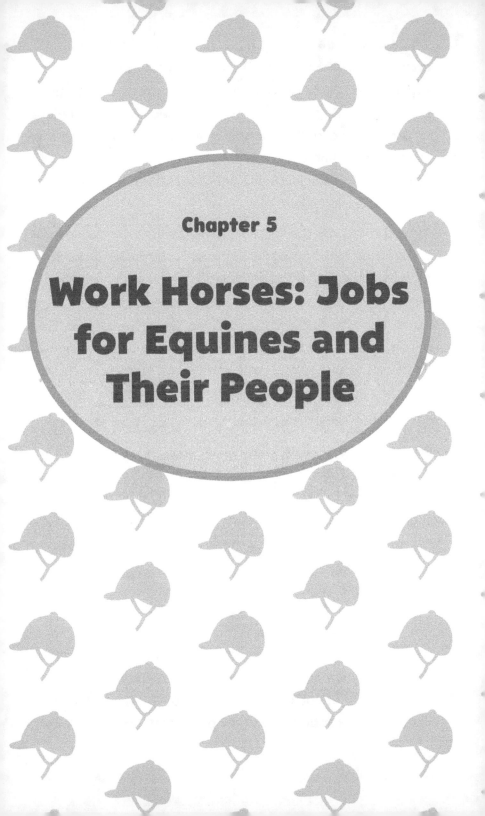

Chapter 5

Work Horses: Jobs for Equines and Their People

What were the small horse-drawn carts that ancient soldiers rode into battle called?

Around 3000 BCE, likely in ancient Mesopotamia (a region in southwestern Asia), a four- or two-wheeled cart pulled by oxen or asses called a chariot was invented. Chariots were likely used in early funeral processions and then came to be used by hunters and soldiers, especially the two-wheeled variety as they were easier to turn.

Around 2000 BCE, the horse took over as the main chariot-pulling draft animal. The people who drove chariots were called charioteers. Chariots also carried other soldiers, sometimes including spearmen. The technology spread all over the old world, including to current-day China, Egypt, India, and Great Britain. Later in ancient times, chariot races became popular and were performed at the ancient Greek Olympics and Roman circus events. Chariots were still in use in the British Isles until the fourth century CE.

Who were knights in medieval times?

Knights were soldiers who were enlisted, trained, and equipped by noblemen and other rich landowners in Europe during the Middle Ages from around 500 to 1500 CE. These knights had to fight in service of the king during wartime and they rode into battle on horses.

What breeds did medieval knights prefer?

Medieval knights were known for wearing heavy, mostly metal armor, so they needed strong, heavy horses to carry them and their armor into battle and during jousting competitions. To learn more about jousting, see chapter 6, "The Inside Track: Horses in Sports and Show," on page 77. Sometimes knights did raids and sieges without armor and used lighter horses though. The Friesian, which originated in the Netherlands, was popular with medieval knights, as were Andalusian, Percheron, and Arabian horses.

In medieval speech, what was a charger?

Charger was another word for a warhorse (a horse that a cavalry soldier used to charge into battle). There were two categories of medieval chargers: heavy destriers that carried armored knights into battle and lighter coursers ridden by unarmored knights during raids.

What group of mounted minutemen originated in Texas in the 1830s?

The Texas Rangers were initially a private militia hired by colonizers to protect settler encampments. They grew into a sort of police force and border patrol and headquartered themselves in Austin, Texas. In 1935, they became part of the Texas Highway Patrol.

What 1872-to-1873 epidemic nearly brought the economy to a halt?

In 1872, an epidemic of equine influenza (equine flu) started in Toronto, Canada, and swept through North and Central America, affecting horses and mules, both essential work animals at the time. An estimated 2 percent of horses died, and many others were too sick to work for weeks.

At the time, everyone relied on horses to transport food, coal, and even industrial materials (but then industry eventually ended up replacing horses with machines). Even though we think of horses as being in the country, cities were especially dependent on horses, since masses of people needed transportation and needed food brought in from agricultural areas. The entire economy was dependent on horses at the time. Prices soared and the economy went into a recession. In some places, undelivered goods piled up, including rotting food.

What disaster in Boston, Massachusetts, was made far worse by the equine flu epidemic?

On November 9, 1872, a fire devastated a large portion of the city of Boston, burning most of the financial district to the ground. However the fire started, the response was too slow because there were no horses to pull the firemen's pump wagons to the scene.

What social movement was fueled by the equine flu epidemic?

There were already animal rights activists before the equine flu. A man named Henry Bergh founded the American Society for the Prevention of Cruelty to Animals in 1866. But the equine flu epidemic made both the suffering of horses and society's debt to them more visible to the public. Some carriage horse owners were making their sick horses continue to work, sometimes to death. This fueled the movement for animal rights.

What were people who stole horses in the Old West called?

Not all professions are legal and good. Rustling was the common term for stealing farm animals, including cattle and horses. An outlaw known as a horse rustler was someone who stole horses. Rustling stories have been fodder for many a Western film. And in the Old West, the penalty could be steep, including hanging!

What's a dude ranch?

A dude ranch is another name for a Western guest ranch where you can stay on vacation and do Western ranching activities. In the early 1900s, the word dude was actually an insult against privileged city folks who came out West to see what life was like there and to pretend to be cowboys. The term is no longer meant negatively, and you can go to dude ranches to experience horse riding, Western dancing, fishing, and other Old West and current Western activities.

What is a cowboy?

A cowboy is a person whose job it is to herd and take care of cattle at a ranch. They do much of their work on horseback, so their horses help to round up the cattle.

How does a cowboy usually hold a horse's reins?

Even though Western-style reins are usually split reins (two separate straps instead of one continuous piece), cowboys tend to hold both reins in the left hand, freeing up the right hand for things like roping cattle. But one Western style of rein holding uses both hands, which you can read about in the next entry.

What are the two main styles of rein holding in Western-style riding?

In Western riding, there are two main styles of holding the reins: traditional and California. In the traditional style, both reins are held only in the left fist with the thumb pointed toward the front of the horse and the right hand free and resting on the right thigh. In California style, the reins are held in the left fist, but the thumb points up toward the sky, and the rest of the rein that's hanging down is held in the right fist that rests on the rider's right thigh. As the name suggests, California style originated in the state of California.

What is a lariat?

A lariat is a lasso (a long rope with a loop at the end) used to capture cattle. Western saddles have a saddle horn, almost like a handle that sticks up, that cowboys can wrap the lariat around to keep a hold of it.

How many horses served in the military during World War II?

Cars began to take over as our primary mode of transportation in the early 1900s, but a few decades in, warhorses, carriage horses, and others were still hard at work all over the world. During World War II, which lasted from 1939 to 1945, as many as eight million horses served alongside humans in the military.

Where do the horses of New York City's mounted police sleep at night?

New York City is one of many with police officers on horseback, known as mounted police. Mounted police work in Central Park and at crowded events. These working horses have to rest and sleep just like the officers, but they don't go home with their riders. There is a special stable in a luxury apartment building near Times Square in midtown Manhattan where the horses go to rest and feed. This stable includes 27 stalls, automatic water feeders, an indoor exercise ring, horse shower facilities, and an on-site farrier (who takes care of the horses' hooves). It is actually one of four stables for mounted police horses in the city.

What human-health-related work do some horses take part in?

Studies have shown that being around pets like cats and dogs can decrease anxiety and be good for people's mental and physical health. And the same goes for horses! In fact, horses are sometimes used along with therapy to help with mental issues like anxiety, depression, behavioral problems, attention deficit hyperactivity disorder, and more. This is called equine therapy or equine-assisted therapy. It involves working with others to care for horses, which apparently helps build self-esteem, self-confidence, and empathy. In the physical health realm, horse riding is also sometimes used as a form of physical therapy.

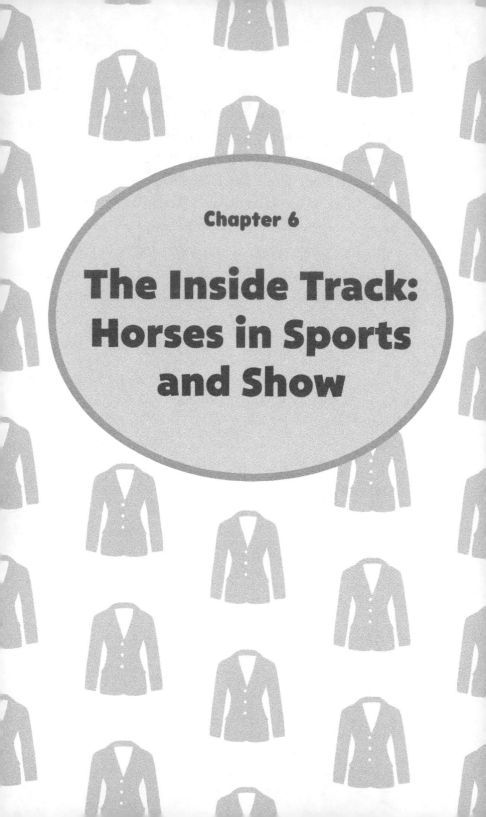

Chapter 6

The Inside Track: Horses in Sports and Show

What is jousting?

One early horse sport was first conducted in medieval Europe from the 11th to the 17th century. Two armor-wearing knights would mount their horses and ride straight at each other holding lances (a long weapon like a spear) with blunt ends and try to knock each other off their horses. Jousting was originally a form of training for battle, but it became a sport, and a very dangerous one. Many knights and royals were injured, or even killed, during the competitions. This includes King Henry II of France, who died in 1559 after part of a broken lance pierced his eye.

What alternative form of jousting was introduced in later medieval times?

A less injurious form of jousting called running or tilting at the ring was introduced in the 1600s. In this competition, the knights still mounted their horses and each carried a lance (this time a shorter one), but instead of using the lance on other knights, they would use the lance to grab and collect three rings hanging from arches in a field. This show of skill had a much lower body count than knight-on-knight jousting, preserving the soldiers for battle.

What US state's official state sport is ring-tournament jousting?

Acting out ancient rites and battles is not uncommon, but real jousting competitions have also been held for quite some time, including in the United States. From the time of its colonization, Maryland has had jousting, introduced by the second Lord Baltimore, who governed the province of Maryland in the 1600s. In 1962, Maryland state senator Henry Fowler, himself a jouster and president of the Maryland Jousting Tournament Association, introduced a bill to make three-ring jousting the state's official sport, and it passed. This made Maryland the first state with an official sport.

What modern word for a temporary worker referred to a certain type of knight?

Nobles generally had their own knights whom they would put into jousting tournaments against the knights of other nobles or send into battle (knights were soldiers, after all). But some knights were not dedicated to one lord and could be hired to compete or fight for anyone. These knights were known as "freelancers," a word we use today to refer to someone doing temporary work for hire rather than being hired as a regular employee.

What do "on the flat" and "over fences" mean in a hunt-seat competition?

Hunt-seat is a style of English riding derived from fox hunting. In competitions for this style of riding, "on the flat" and "over fences" have to do with judging riders and their horses during two different types of activity. Judging "on the flat" means the competitors are being rated for their skills at different gaits in a flat arena. Judging "over fences" means they are being rated for skills on a course with jumps.

What is dressage?

Dressage is the training of horses to perform specific movements for show that range from simple gaits to acrobatics. There are competitions in dressage, including in the Olympics. Dressage looks a lot like dancing and is super fun to watch!

In competitive dressage, what are the mastery levels?

It is possible to attain the following levels in dressage: introductory level, training level, first level, second level, third level, fourth level, and Olympic level.

In horse riding, what is "impulsion"?

Impulsion is a term used in dressage for a horse using its hind legs to propel itself forward (and a little upward) in a controlled way.

What are the "airs above the ground" in dressage?

The "airs above the ground" are a group of dressage movements in which the horse's feet leave the ground, sometimes for a few seconds. The three most famous and currently performed movements are as follows:

- **Levade:** The horse bends its hocks (knee joints) nearly to the ground, raises its front legs off the ground, and holds its body at a 45-degree angle for a few moments

- **Courbette:** The horse stands on its hind legs, lifts its front legs off the ground, and jumps forward on its hind legs more than once

- **Capriole:** The horse leaps into the air, tucking its front legs and kicking its back legs straight out like it's flying

Most dressage shows do not involve these difficult moves, but read about one school and breed of horses that are still famous for performing the "airs above the ground" next.

What breed of horse was made famous for its ability to perform the "airs above the ground" in dressage?

The Lipizzaner horse, also called the Lipizzan horse or the Spanish horse (despite actually being from Austria), was made famous by the Spanish Riding School in Vienna, Austria, whose horses are known for their acrobatic dressage performances. The performing Spanish Riding School horses are sometimes called the "white stallions" because they appear to be white after a certain age. They are born with dark coloring that lightens over time to what is actually a very light gray. Read on to find out more about these majestic and athletic horses.

Why are Lipizzaners referred to as Spanish horses, or Lipizzaners, for that matter?

Lipizzaners were first bred by a 16th-century archduke named Karl II Franz who ruled in an area known at the time as Inner Austria (later incorporated into Italy). His original farm where he bred horses was in Lipica—in Italian the name is Lipizza. As for the term Spanish horse, from the 8th to the 15th century, horses from Spain were crossbred with Arabian horses, ultimately leading to the Lipizzaner created by the archduke.

The breed had the intelligence, strength, and agility necessary to learn and perform acrobatic dressage moves, including the "airs above the ground" for which they are famous. The Spanish Riding School is named for the horses, not for its location. The school and breeding farm moved several times due to European wars and is now located outside of Vienna, Austria. And the town of Lipica where the breed originated is now part of Slovenia. Borders are ever changing.

What is the half-seat position?

Also known as the two-point position, the half-seat position is the pose the rider is supposed to take while their horse is jumping. It involves lifting out of the saddle while leaning the body forward over the horse's neck. Riders have to be able to do this to do well in English-riding jumping competitions.

When was the first annual rodeo held?

Rodeos are events where cowboys can showcase their horse riding, cow roping, and other skills. The name comes from the Spanish word *rodear*, which means "to encircle." The first annually held rodeo began on July 4, 1888, in Prescott, Arizona Territory. Rodeos are still put on today. They include such events as bareback bronc riding, barrel racing, team roping, and bull riding.

What is a cutting competition?

Cutting is a Western-style cowboy event in which a horse and its rider are judged by how well they separate (or "cut") a single cow from its herd and keep it from going back to the herd.

Why are Western saddles larger and more padded than English saddles?

Western saddles were developed for the rigors of a cowboy's life on the range, which includes riding for a much longer time (often all day) to round up cattle. This makes comfort and stability key. This extra material also usually makes Western saddles heavier than English saddles.

What is barrel racing?

Barrel racing is a Western-style equestrian sport in which riders race their horses around three barrels in a sort of cloverleaf pattern for a set amount of time.

What is a bronc in rodeo events?

A bronc (or bronco) is an untamed horse used in Western-style saddle-bronc and bareback-bronc events. In these events, the riders are judged for their ability to ride and stay on a bronc who, not used to being ridden, is often bucking and trying to throw off its rider.

In what region did polo originate?

One sport people play while riding horses is polo, during which horse riders attempt to hit a ball through a goal using long wooden mallets. Although it became a sport of the upper class in England, the sport originated in northwest India in the state of Manipur sometime in the 1800s. Great Britain colonized (took control of) India, and British soldiers stationed there brought the sport back with them.

What are the six separate segments of a polo match called?

Polo matches are broken up into segments of 7½ minutes called chukka, or chukkers.

What item of clothing is named for polo?

An item of clothing that is popular to this day is the polo shirt, although in its current form, its origins owe more to tennis than to polo. People used to play polo (and tennis) in long-sleeve, button-down dress shirts, the types you might see on a businessperson today. These weren't very practical for sports though. Polo players used to pin down their collars so they didn't flap while they rode. So the Brooks Brothers company created something it called a polo shirt in 1896. It had a button-down collar, but it was still like a dress shirt and didn't allow for a good range of motion.

In the 1920s, French tennis player Jean René Lacoste created a lightweight, short-sleeve tennis shirt with a collar and three buttons at the top. He also embroidered a small alligator on the upper-left chest area. He cofounded the clothing company Lacoste, which made the shirts for the public. He later licensed the shirt to Izod in 1951, which still produces the Izod Lacoste shirt. Polo players started wearing what we now call polo shirts around the 1950s. In 1972, Ralph Lauren began producing his cotton polo shirts with an embroidered polo player, which are also still available.

What is a hunter-pace competition?

This is a type of cross-country race in which a trail is marked through a natural landscape that includes terrain and obstacles typical of fox hunting. The trail is usually around 6 miles long. Rather than hunting a fox, the aim is to ride the trail and have your team finish with the best time that is considered safe for the horses and riders.

What are Horse Trials?

Also called the "three-day event," and often just referred to as "eventing," the horse trials are a three-day event during which a rider and their horse compete in certain events each day. The first-day competition is dressage. The second day is a cross-country race with jumps. The third day is arena show jumping. Eventing used to be called the "militaire" because it was intended to test the abilities of cavalry horses.

What is a gymkhana?

Gymkhanas are show-riding events in which children are the competitors or that feature all-age events in which children are allowed to also compete. Gymkhana events can include timed events like barrel racing, keyhole racing, pole bending, and figure-eight competitions, as well as things like the egg-and-spoon race. And some include fancy dress competitions, in which riders and their ponies get to dress up in costumes!

What sort of event combines horse riding and gymnastics?

Vaulting is a very acrobatic horse-related sport. Unlike in dressage—in which the horses are performing the acrobatics—in vaulting, it's the humans doing acrobatics. Vaulting often involves a handler controlling the horse's movements with a longe line (like a very long leash) while the rider performs a series of gymnastic-type moves on the back of the horse with the help of special handles on a pad strapped to the horse. Vaulting competitors are judged on a series of required movements, a freestyle performance, and their mounting and dismounting skills. And the horses get judged for their gaits.

What equestrian events are included in the Olympic Games?

The current Olympic Games include three equestrian events: dressage, show jumping, and three-day eventing. The first two take place in an arena, and the third is an outdoor cross-country event of up to 4 miles in length. Fun fact: The original Olympics in ancient Greece also included horse racing and chariot racing.

Who was the first non-Australian to win the Melbourne Cup?

The Melbourne Cup is a famous annual horse race held in Australia. Dermot Weld (from Ireland) and his horse Vintage Crop won the Melbourne Cup in 1993.

What is the rider in a horse race called?

The person who rides a horse during a horse race is called a jockey.

What is the purse in horse racing?

The purse is the money awarded to the winner of the horse race. Currently, the largest purse in the world is for the Dubai World Cup, whose winner gets a whopping $10 million!

In what sort of arena horse race does the horse have to jump obstacles on the course?

Most horse racing is around a flat track in an arena. But another popular form of horse racing is the steeplechase, in which the horses and their jockeys race around a course and jump over obstacles, including fences, ditches, and water jumps. The horses in these races are referred to as chasers. The race got its name from a tradition in Ireland, where riders would race their horses from church steeple to church steeple across obstacle-covered terrain.

What is the Triple Crown?

The Triple Crown is more of an achievement than an event. Three major horse races in the United States are involved: the Kentucky Derby, the Preakness Stakes, and the Belmont Stakes—all races for 3-year-old Thoroughbreds. A horse who wins all three in the same season is said to have won the Triple

Crown. Only 13 horses have won it since its inception in 1875. The first winner was Sir Barton in 1919. Another was the famous racehorse Secretariat in 1973.

What famous racehorse's skeleton was displayed at the American Museum of Natural History?

From 1904 to 1906, the racehorse Sysonby had a winning streak, but sadly he died in 1906 at the young age of 4 years and 4 months old. The horse's remains were donated to the American Museum of Natural History in New York. In 1908, the museum had the horse's skeleton mounted in a racing stride and put on display. Currently the skeleton is in storage at the museum.

What day of a famous British horse-racing event prompts people to dress up, often in extravagant hats?

The three-day annual Grand National races at the Aintree Racecourse in Aintree, near Liverpool, England, is one of the most famous horse-racing events in the world. But one day of the event gets attention worldwide for more than just the races. The first day of the event is called Ladies Day. A time-honored tradition on this day is for people to dress in formal, often colorful clothes, especially the women, who sometimes also wear large, fancy hats. Celebrities and royal family members are usually in attendance.

What horse won the Grand National three times in the 1970s?

Red Rum won the Grand National in 1973, 1974, and 1977.

What is harness racing?

In harness racing, horses race around the track pulling small, short, two-wheeled carts called sulkies with a driver aboard.

What is the Hambletonian Stakes?

The Hambletonian Stakes, also known as the Hambletonian Trot, is a major harness racing event in the United States. Originally run in Syracuse, New York, in 1926, the race has moved a few times and is now held at the Meadowlands Racetrack in New Jersey. The equine competitors are all three-year-old trotters.

What is the Extreme Mustang Makeover Challenge?

No, it doesn't involve putting makeup on a horse. The Extreme Mustang Makeover Challenge is an event in which feral horses who have been living in Bureau of Land Management corrals are assigned to trainers and taught new skills over 100 days. They then participate in a competition to demonstrate the skills, after which they are sold in an auction.

What event uses Genghis Khan's ancient postal stations as its route markers?

The Mongol Derby is a 1,000-kilometer (about 620 miles) horse race in Mongolia held annually. At that distance, it is the longest horse race in the world, according to Guinness World Records. People come from all over the world to participate, and they pay a hefty entry fee of over $13,000 per rider (much of it to cover costs of emergency services and horse care).

But the riders don't bring their own horses. Participants are provided with local Mongolian horses given to them at stations at the start of each leg of the race. These stations are called *urtuu* (or *yams*), which are postal-horse relay stations of the sort used by the Mongolian postal service in the time of Genghis Khan (the ruler of the Mongol Empire that included parts of China and central Asia early in the 13th century). In fact, the race covers areas that were part of this ancient postal service. The riders have little control over what horse they get at each station, and they might not be able to ride the same horse all the way through. The safety of the horses is taken seriously, and horses are not allowed to leave the station until they cool down and their heart rate comes down to a safe speed. Some of the wily horses do not behave, and the terrain of the Mongolian steppe, while beautiful, can be harsh, so falls and other mishaps are common. Although no one has died, there have been many broken bones and other injuries.

In what activity do competitors ride fake horses?

Hobbyhorsing is a competitive event that originated in Finland. It consists of dressage and jumping events—with a twist. Rather than riding a real horse, the rider is astride a hobbyhorse that consists of a stick with a plush toy horse head on the end. You may have seen similar toys in stores, but the heads of competitive hobbyhorses are usually a little more detailed and slightly larger than the typical child's toy. The sport and its competitive events are organized by the Finnish Hobbyhorse Association. The horses are given names by their riders, and both the riders' and horses' names are called out during competitions. Some of the hobbyhorses have tails. Some have braided hair and some free-hanging manes. Some of the riders even make their own hobbyhorses. In hobbyhorsing, it is the rider doing the acrobatics. It's fun and exercise! *Hobbyhorse Revolution*, a documentary film about the sport, was released in 2018.

Chapter 7

The Horse and Buggy Days: History of the Horse

What is the oldest known text on horse care and training?

A set of four clay tablets called *The Kikkuli Text* is the first known manual about the care, feeding, and training of horses. The tablets date from around 1345 BCE and are named for the horse trainer Kikkuli, who took care of chariot horses. The tablets are written in an alphabet known as cuneiform. They were found by an archaeologist (someone who studies materials from past civilizations) in 1906 in what is now central Turkey.

What is the oldest known text on dressage and horsemanship?

Xenophon was an ancient Greek historian and cavalryman who studied with the famous Greek philosopher Socrates. He lived from 431 to 354 BCE. Xenophon wrote a book called *On Horsemanship*. The book includes advice on buying and training horses both for war and for show.

What famous horse was ridden by Alexander the Great?

Alexander the Great ruled Macedonia (a region in southern Europe) starting in 336 BCE and greatly expanded the empire before his early death. His horse Bucephalus was a sort of horse celebrity of the ancient world. The horse was reportedly black with a white star on his face. Legend had it that Bucephalus was untamable until Alexander tamed him as a boy. In the story, Alexander used the fact that the horse was afraid of his shadow to his advantage by turning the horse's face toward the sun so he could mount him. Bucephalus died in 326 BCE in the Battle of the Hydaspes, and Alexander named a city (possibly what is now Jhelum, Pakistan) Bucephala in his horse's honor. Alexander died just three years later in 323 BCE.

What Roman general (later turned emperor) reportedly sent away his army's horses when he thought victory was doubtful in an upcoming battle?

According the Roman biographer Suetonius in his work *De vita Caesarum* (commonly called *Lives of the Caesars* or *The Twelve Caesars* today), when Julius Caesar was in command of the Roman forces, he would send away the horses, including his own. He did this so the soldiers would have no means of escape and therefore a greater need to stand their ground and win. Suetonius also said that Caesar's horse was bred by Caesar himself and had hooves that were divided so they resembled human toes, although unfortunately he didn't mention the name of this horse.

What Roman emperor was said to have been planning to make one of his horses a government official?

Caligula, the Roman emperor from 37 to 41 CE, has a reputation for cruel, excessive, and eccentric behavior. Some of it is likely exaggeration but has been preserved by historians who wrote about him decades after his reign. One of these historians was Suetonius, who wrote in his work *Lives of the Caesars* that Caligula lavishly housed and fed his beloved horse Incitatus, and he even planned to elevate him to consul, a high government post. Caligula's assassination (murder for political reasons) less than four years into his time as ruler reportedly put a stop to the plan. Whether true or not, it is a colorful story.

What was the Parthian shot?

In the third century BCE, the soldiers from Parthia (in modern-day Iran) pioneered an effective horseback war tactic. They rode away from the enemy, and when the enemy followed after them, they turned 180 degrees in their saddles and shot arrows back at the enemy pursuers. They managed to do this without stirrups and controlled the horses with their legs!

Where were horseshoes invented?

Historians aren't entirely sure where horseshoes first originated. Two possibilities are China in the third century BCE or Rome sometime before the first century BCE. The Roman poet Catullus mentions a mule losing a shoe around that time. Over time, they became more and more widespread, especially starting around 1000 CE. In medieval times, from around 500 to 1500 CE, horseshoes were made by blacksmiths. Now they are churned out by machines.

Horseshoes are shaped like a letter *u* that curves in at the top. Because horseshoes are so well known, many things with the same shape are described as horseshoe shaped, for instance, horseshoe crabs and horseshoe-backed armchairs. There's even a game called horseshoes in which people throw either actual horseshoes or horseshoe-shaped objects at stakes in the ground.

What ancient warlord used horses to conquer the largest landmass ever?

Genghis Khan was a Mongolian ruler in the 13th century who used horse-driven warfare to take over most of Asia, Russia, and the Middle East. This makes the Mongolian empire the largest connected empire in history—even to this day! In most countries and regions of the world, horse-mounted cavalry made up only a part of each military force. But in the armies of Genghis Khan, every single soldier was on horseback, which made them incredibly fast and mobile compared to other armies. It probably didn't hurt that horses were first domesticated around northern Mongolia and were still very prevalent in the area.

Genghis Khan also made trade routes between Asia, the Middle East, and Europe safer for travel and trade. His empire lasted over 100 years, maintained by his descendants, including his grandson Kublai Khan. The Khans also instituted a system that allowed for fast communication between people. See the next entry to learn more.

What communication network did Genghis Khan set up?

Genghis Khan used horses to take over a huge area, but he also used them to set up a fast and vast postal system that spanned thousands of miles. His postal system consisted of horse relay stations, called *urtuu* or *yams*, every 50 miles or so. Postal riders and other travelers could stop at them for food, water, and rest, and the postal carriers could get new horses to more easily continue their long journeys. Runners on foot and boats were also employed in the system. According to Marco Polo, an Italian explorer who traveled to Asia in the late 1200s, there were around 10,000 relay stations in Asia during the rule of Kublai Khan. It wasn't the first postal system, but it was by far the fastest. The bubonic plague interrupted the original postal system in the 1340s, and the Mongolian horse-driven postal service was completely shut down in 1949 by the Soviet Union, then in control of Mongolia.

What famous postal system in the United States used horses for transit during a brief period in the 1800s?

The Pony Express was a short-lived attempt at fast postal delivery mainly on horseback that spanned about 2,000 miles from St. Joseph, Missouri, to Sacramento, California. The Pony Express lasted only from April 1860 to October 1861. It was meant to speed up delivery, which at the time could take nearly a month. By using similar methods to Genghis Khan's system, including relay stations with riders changing horses frequently, it managed a delivery time of 10 days over the whole route. One of its riders was "Buffalo Bill" Cody, famous for his Wild West show. The Pony Express was shut down when the transcontinental telegraph line was completed, making the expensive enterprise unnecessary.

What invention enabled the creation of the first reliable vehicles faster than horses?

Horses have given humans a form of fast transportation from the time they were domesticated over 6,000 years ago. But in 1698, an invention gave them a run for their money: the steam engine. It took a while but by the early 1800s, the steam engine was used to power ships and trains, vehicles that competed with horse-driven transportation.

What was the famous O.K. Corral?

There are many famous stories about the shootout at the O.K. Corral between law enforcement officials led by Virgil Earp and the outlaw group the Cowboys. But few, if any, actually say what the O.K. Corral was. It was, in fact, a place in Tombstone, Arizona, where cowboys could unsaddle and leave their horses for a rest, watering, and feeding while they took care of other business. Kind of like doggie daycare, but for horses.

What category of horse became rare after the transition to an industrial economy?

The US and a lot of other countries used to have economies based on agriculture (or farming). Especially in the age before motors were everywhere, there were many more draft horses. They pulled plows and other farm equipment, and they pulled carriages to transport people and goods. But when cars, tractors, and other fuel-powered vehicles became common, the need for draft horses to pull heavy things for humans decreased drastically, and so did the population of draft horses. The horses were still used for a while to haul goods during the transition, however. Before cars and other mechanical transportation were everywhere, horses were needed to haul industrial materials. Some of them hauled materials for the machines that ultimately replaced them.

What type of horse did a major beer company use to mark the end of Prohibition in the US?

In 1920, the 18th Amendment to the United States Constitution banned the manufacture or sale of alcohol in the United States. This was called Prohibition and was, of course, upsetting to liquor and beer companies. In 1933, the 21st Amendment to the Constitution ended Prohibition.

In April 1933, the sons of Augustus A. Busch Sr. presented their father with a team of six Clydesdale horses to celebrate the repeal. Thinking this was a good advertising idea, they bought another six Clydesdales and had them pull a beer wagon through New York City to the Empire State Building, where they presented a case of Budweiser to the governor of New York. The horse team toured the East Coast that month and stopped in Washington, DC, to deliver another case to President Franklin Delano Roosevelt. The Clydesdales have been a part of the Anheuser-Busch company ever since. In 1950, the company also introduced a dalmatian dog as a mascot of the horses, and a dalmatian still travels with each group of Clydesdales.

What were hansom cabs?

These days we hail a taxicab (or an Uber) if we need a lift. But back before cars, cabs were horse-drawn carriages. Early horse-drawn cabs weren't always very stable and would sometimes tip over. In 1834, Joseph Hansom, an architect from York, England, designed and patented a safety cab that was more stable but just as fast as other cabs of the time. It had two wheels and could be pulled by only one horse. Rather than sitting at the front, the driver sat at the back of the carriage in a high seat and talked to the passengers through an open sunroof.

Hansom sold the patent (an official document stating who has the rights to an invention) for the design to a company for 10,000 British pounds, but sadly they never paid him. Others improved and repatented the design, and hansom cabs (still named for their original creator) became very popular in cities like London, Paris, Berlin, and New York. Like most horse-pulled transportation, they were replaced by cars. The last London hansom cabdriver retired his cab in 1947.

What horse breed took over for women and child coal miners when labor laws were changed in Britain?

Before 1847 in Britain, men, women, and children alike worked deep in mines hauling up the coal used as fuel. That year, a law was passed that banned women and children from working in the mines. To replace the labor force, mine owners enlisted Shetland ponies to work with the male coal miners and haul loads out of the mines. The last coal-mining pony retired in 1994.

What labor organization came out of the struggles of carriage drivers?

The International Brotherhood of Teamsters, often just called the Teamsters, is a labor union protecting worker's rights in a wide variety of jobs today. But it started out to protect, and is named for, teamsters. Teamsters were people who drove horse-driven vehicles. The name refers to driving a team (two or more) of horses. Before cars, these drivers and their horses and carriages were a major form of transportation in the world for both people and goods like food and building materials. Teamster can also mean truck driver (a profession that replaced horse driving when cars became widespread).

What war was fought over horses?

In the second century BCE in China, Emperor Wu of Han (during the Han dynasty that ruled China for more than 400 years) began importing horses from the Dayuan people of Ferghana (now part of Uzbekistan) to supply his cavalry. The Ferghana horses, called "heavenly" horses, were known for their short, muscular stature and for what was thought to be their trait of sweating blood (in fact, it was likely a skin condition caused by a parasite). The Dayuan people decided China was importing too many of its horses, so they cut off the supply. Around 102 to 104 BCE, China fought Ferghana over the horse dispute in a conflict dubbed the War of the Heavenly Horses. China ultimately took over the region and restarted the horse trade. The Ferghana breed sadly is now extinct (no longer exists).

What ancient trade route got part of its name from horses?

The Tea Horse Road in China is an ancient trade route that may have been formed as early as 2,000 years ago. Although horses helped carry the goods (including a lot of tea, but also silk and salt), that's not exactly why the path has "horse" in its name. It's called the Tea Horse Road because some traders would swap tea for Tibetan ponies needed for both hauling and war.

Where can you find Napoleon Bonaparte's last horse?

The Arabian horse Le Vizir was given to Napoleon Bonaparte, the emperor of France in the early 1800s, by an Ottoman (Turkish) sultan in 1802. Le Vizir's taxidermied (stuffed and mounted) remains are on display at Le Musée de l'Armée in Paris, France. It's located right next to Les Invalides, a former military hospital that is now also a museum and the final resting place of Napoleon's remains.

Who was the lone member of the US Cavalry found alive after the Battle of the Little Bighorn?

In 1876, General George Armstrong Custer led the US Seventh Cavalry to a massive defeat in a battle against Cheyenne and Lakota Sioux warriors at the Battle of the Little Bighorn. It is also known as Custer's Last Stand, as the entire regiment was wiped out. But a lone survivor was found on the field after the battle: a horse named Comanche. The horse's rider, Captain Miles Keough, didn't make it. And Comanche himself was seriously wounded, having been shot seven times. But the horse was taken to Fort Abraham Lincoln in the Dakota Territory and nursed back to health.

In 1878, Comanche was retired and lived out the rest of his days in comfort as the mascot of the Seventh Cavalry. He died in 1890 and became the first horse given a funeral with full military honors. His remains were put on display at the University of Kansas's Natural History Museum. Comanche probably wasn't the only horse to survive the Battle of the Little Bighorn. Others are thought to have survived and fled the scene.

What photographic experiment with horses led to the invention of motion pictures?

Around 1872, railroad tycoon (a wealthy, powerful business-person) Leland Stanford wanted to prove that all four of a racehorse's legs left the ground at once during its fast gaits. He hired a photographer named Eadweard J. Muybridge to prove it. It took years, but Muybridge developed a camera shutter that could capture an image with an exposure of only 0.002 second (in other words, it would take 500 times that to equal one second). Using up to 24 cameras at once, he photographed a jockey riding a horse and proved Stanford right. Muybridge also invented a device called the zoopraxiscope that projected images of photographs on a spinning glass disc by shining light through them to demonstrate his findings. Fun fact: That device was an important predecessor to modern film projectors, so horses played a major role in the invention of movies!

Who invented a sidesaddle that held the rider's legs in place?

The sidesaddle is thought to have been invented in 1382, when Anne of Bohemia rode across Europe to marry King Richard II of England. Early sidesaddles were basically sideways seats on horses. Women couldn't face forward and their legs either dangled from the side of the horse or were placed on a foot-rest. This gave them little control of the horse, and they tended to fall off. In 1580, Catherine de Medici (the queen of King Henry II of France) is said to have invented a sidesaddle that held the rider's legs in place with a stirrup for the left foot and a pommel (or raised spot on the saddle) to hold the right leg in place, giving sidesaddle riders more stability and control. Later innovations made sidesaddle riding even more stable. Eventually it was no longer considered improper for a woman to sit with her legs on either side of a horse, and using sidesaddles fell out of favor.

During World War II, what group of horses did US forces go out of their way to save?

During World War II, Alois Podhajsky, an Austrian colonel, was in charge of the Spanish Riding School in Vienna, Austria. This is where the famous Lipizzaner horses performed the acrobatic movements described in chapter 6, "The Inside Track: Horses in Sports and Show," on page 80. The school was temporarily relocated to Upper Austria, and the German high command had the Lipizzaner breeding stock moved to a town in Czechoslovakia (now the Czech Republic).

In May 1945, Germany surrendered, and Russian troops were approaching Czechoslovakia, which had been made part of their territory. US troops had just captured the school and requested a show for the US general George Patton. At the end of the show, Podhajsky asked Patton for protection for the show horses and retrieval of the breeding horses.

Patton's Second Cavalry Group sent someone behind enemy lines to the stud farm to negotiate surrender. The US military took over the farm and rescued hundreds of horses (including around 250 Lipizzaners) and over a thousand prisoners of war the Germans had been holding in the area, some of whom took care of the horses.

In a mission called Operation Cowboy, the US Army transported the horses to safety in Mansbach, Germany, about 130 miles away, and shortly after, the Lipizzaners were returned to Austria. Podhajsky staged performances of the Spanish Riding School for US soldiers for months after that. And you can still see the horses perform today!

Who founded the International League for the Protection of Horses?

In 1911, a British woman named Ada Cole saw British draft horses being whipped on their way to a slaughterhouse in Belgium. She started lobbying (taking actions to try to influence members of the government) and fundraising to prevent people from exporting British horses to be slaughtered. In 1927, she founded the International League for the Protection of Horses, which is still around under the name World Horse Welfare and now works to prevent cruelty to horses worldwide.

Who was Wild Horse Annie?

Velma Bronn Johnston, also known as Wild Horse Annie, was an animal rights activist starting in the 1950s, when she saw blood dripping from a truck on the road and found out it was carrying mustangs to slaughter. Her campaigns (a series of actions to get a specific result) against the capture and killing of feral horses and burros—like having children write letters to the government—led to legislation protecting them.

What is the name of the horse Queen Elizabeth II of England rode nearly every day?

Queen Elizabeth II of England rode a royal Fell pony named Carltonlima Emma.

Where do Brumbies roam free?

Brumbies are a feral population of horses that roam free in Australia. They are considered by many to be an invasive species that is damaging the ecosystems they inhabit, although some people want to preserve them. There were an estimated 14,000 brumbies in Australia as of 2021, but there has been talk of culling them down to just 3,000 in number.

When did a horse first set foot (or hoof) in Australia?

Horses are not native to Australia. In fact, no hard-hoofed animals are. The first horses to arrive in Australia were brought by Western colonizers (settlers who took control of the country) in 1788.

What famous "bob-tail nag" is referenced in the song "Camptown Races"?

The 1859 song "Camptown Races" by Stephen Foster includes the line "I'll bet my money on de bob-tail nag." The "bob-tail nag" was racehorse Flora Temple. She lived from 1845 to 1877 and is famous for having won 92 races and being the second mare to trot the mile in under 2 minutes and 30 seconds. In

1955, she was inducted into the Harness Racing Hall of Fame's Hall of Immortals.

Who was the first mare to run the mile in under 2 minutes 30 seconds?

The Thoroughbred Lady Suffolk lived from 1833 to 1855. She pulled an oyster cart before she was purchased and put to work as a racehorse. She ran the mile in 2 minutes and 29.5 seconds, the first mare to do so. She also won two out of three of her races. Lady Suffolk was inducted into the Harness Racing Hall of Fame's Hall of Immortals in 1967.

What horse became famous for his display of astounding math and spelling skills?

William Key was born into slavery in 1833 in Shelbyville, Tennessee. He always had a love of horses, and he became a self-taught horse trainer and veterinarian. He bought an Arabian circus horse named Lauretta who was pregnant with the foal of a standardbred racehorse named Tennessee Volunteer. He planned to race the unborn horse, but Jim Key (the name given the foal) was sickly and clumsy and not racehorse material.

But the horse was beloved—and even slept in the house. And he turned out to have other talents. William and his wife noticed that the horse was picking up tricks from their dog and could nod yes and shake his head no to certain questions, like asking if he wanted an apple (to which he would, of course, nod yes). William taught him to do other tricks like spell and count (demonstrated by placing numbers and letters on an upright rack), use a cash register, sort mail, and tell time! William took Jim on the road to demonstrate the horse's abilities. Whether he was merely performing tricks or had really mastered spelling, he was a remarkable horse and at some point was given the name Beautiful Jim Key. William Key and his business partner took Jim on the road with a play called *The Scholar and the Model Office Boy*, and they demonstrated Jim's abilities at the 1904 St. Louis World's Fair. Both were staunch animal rights activists who pushed for training animals with kindness rather than cruelty. William started the Jim Key Band of Mercy organization and got over two million children to sign the Jim Key Pledge to be kind to animals. William Key passed away in 1909 and Beautiful Jim Key, in 1912.

What horse was famous for its flying tail?

A golden palomino horse later named Nautical started life in 1944 at a ranch in New Mexico, which is why he had a brand on his neck. His original name was an offensive Native American slur. He went through several owners and trainers and was known to be difficult to handle. In 1955, Hugh Wiley was asked to compete for the US Equestrian Team and told he would need two horses. He had one and set about looking for another and was pointed to this horse that he renamed Nautical.

Over his career, Nautical and his rider won and placed in several competitions, including winning the King George V Gold Cup at the Royal International Horse Show of Great Britain in 1959. He was known for his tail, which would jump as he jumped, pleasing the crowd. Nautical was retired in 1960 and lived out the last six years of his life as a normal horse. Also in 1960, Disney released a partially fictional, partially true documentary about Nautical called *The Horse with the Flying Tail*. And the Breyer company made a model horse toy replica of Nautical.

In what competition did an American temporarily take the place of an Irish rider so that Ireland could compete?

During international competitions held in 1950 by the US Equestrian Team in the US, Ireland didn't have enough riders to compete due to injuries. In a show of good sportsmanship, the US Equestrian Team drew names and loaned rider Hugh Wiley to them (later famous for riding Nautical). Ireland won that year.

Who was Seabiscuit?

Seabiscuit was a famous racehorse during the 1930s in the United States. He was grandson to famous racehorse Man o' War but didn't have much of a winning streak in his early career. He was badly treated, over-raced, underfed, and whipped. A new owner, Charles Howard, and new trainer took a more humane approach, feeding him better hay, letting him sleep in, and providing him with a horse companion named Pumpkin. A dog named Pocatell and a spider monkey named Jo-Jo also moved in with the horses.

Seabiscuit began winning races, even beating a son of Man o' War named War Admiral in a surprise defeat in 1938. He suffered a ligament injury but recovered and made a comeback, winning another major race in 1940. He's had movies made about him, including a 1949 Shirley Temple film called *The Story of Seabiscuit* and a 2003 film with Tobey Maguire simply called *Seabiscuit*. Charles Howard even made a 1939 documentary about his horse.

Chapter 8

Horseplay: Arts, Entertainment, and Toys

What early artworks show horses more than any other animal?

Prehistoric drawings found on the walls of caves across Europe, with most in Spain and France, depict various animals that prehistoric man encountered, including wooly mammoths, steppe bison, rhinos, and horses. Some cave drawings date from 65,000 years ago when Neanderthals still existed, but most of the art is less than 40,000 years old after *Homo sapiens* became the main, and eventually only, species of human. Around one-third of the animals painted on the cave walls are horses.

What artwork is called the "Panel of Horses"?

Speaking of cave drawings, in 1994 some cave explorers discovered what are now called the Chauvet caves at Vallon-Pont-d'Arc in Ardèche, France. There they encountered spectacular cave drawings of animals that were made 30,000 to 32,000 years ago by Cro-Magnon people during the Paleolithic era. One section of these drawings features horned bison, rhinoceroses (including two fighting each other), and four horse heads in profile. The four horse heads were drawn on top of portions of the other art and appear in a row, one on top of the next, above the fighting rhinos. This section of wall art is known as the "Panel of Horses."

What is the Uffington White Horse?

The Uffington White Horse is a 374-foot-long abstract horse image in the village of Uffington in Oxfordshire, England. The image is cut into the ground up to a meter deep and filled with chalk crushed into a paste. You can only see the horse from overhead. It is thought to have been created between 1400 and 600 BCE during either the Bronze Age or Iron Age—around 3,000 years ago! It is still around because people in the area add new chalk and maintain the original lines of the monument to this day.

What mythological horse helped destroy an ancient city?

According to ancient Greek poetry and mythology, after 10 years of fighting the walled city of Troy in what we call the Trojan Wars, the ancient Greek armies built a giant wooden horse. They left it as a gift outside the gates of Troy and pretended to sail away. The Trojans took the giant horse into the city. What they didn't know was that Greek soldiers hid inside. At night, the soldiers left the horse and opened the city gates to let the Greek armies in. Troy was destroyed, and Greece won the war. And now when someone calls something a "Trojan horse," they mean something that conceals something else. It is often used to mean malware (harmful software) that is snuck into your computer inside other seemingly normal software.

What's the name of the famous flying horse from ancient Greek mythology?

In ancient Greek mythology, the hero Perseus slayed Medusa, the Gorgon with snakes for hair who turned men to stone if they looked at her. The winged horse Pegasus was born out of her blood and later tamed and ridden by Greek hero Bellerophon. One of the constellations (a grouping of starts) was named after Pegasus.

What creature in ancient Greek mythology was half man and half horse?

The centaur is a mythological creature said to have the upper body of a human and the lower body of a horse.

What creature in Scottish mythology was reported to appear as a horse and lure people to their deaths?

The kelpie is a shape-shifting creature in Scottish mythology that was said to often appear as a horse. In the myth, once a person touched the kelpie, they would become stuck and the kelpie would drag them into the river and eat them.

What mythological creature does a famous New Zealand horse named George play on TV and in film?

George, a mixed-breed horse in New Zealand, is periodically fitted with a fake horn so he can play a unicorn on television and in movies, including a Cadbury candy commercial and the 2005 movie *The Chronicles of Narnia: The Lion, the Witch, and the Wardrobe*. The horn is attached by shaving a bit of his hair and applying nontoxic glue.

What legendary group of knights served King Arthur?

In the legends and tales of King Arthur, he enlisted a group of knights referred to as the Knights of the Round Table, named for the round table Arthur was said to have them all sit around to affirm their equality (since there was no head of the table). You can read tales about King Arthur, his knights, and their trusty horses in many books, such as *Le Morte d'Arthur* by Sir Thomas Malory, *The Once and Future King* by T. H. White, and

Mary Stewart's *Arthurian Saga* that starts with the novel *The Crystal Cave*.

What animated Disney film was based on a section of *The Once and Future King* by T. H. White?

The 1963 Disney movie *The Sword in the Stone* was based on the first section of T. H. White's novel *The Once and Future King* (the section was also called "The Sword in the Stone"). The book and cartoon detail young Arthur's training by the wizard Merlin, including transforming into animals, and the pulling of the sword from the stone, the act that made him king.

What 18th-century artist from Liverpool was best known for his horse paintings?

George Stubbs was born in 1724 in Liverpool, England. He taught himself to paint and at first did portraits of people. He studied anatomy (the science of the structure of living things) and later switched to painting realistic horses, some in hunting and horse-racing scenarios. In 1766, he produced an illustrated book called *The Anatomy of the Horse*.

What famous 18th-century book featured a civilization of intelligent horses?

In the fourth section of *Gulliver's Travels* by Jonathan Swift, the main character ends up in the land of the Houyhnhnms, an advanced civilization of horses. In a role reversal, these horses use uncivilized humans called Yahoos as beasts of burden. The horses speak in a language of neighs (including the name Houyhnhnms).

What famous 19th-century novel was written from the point of view of a horse?

The 1877 novel *Black Beauty* by Anna Sewell was written from the point of view of a black horse whose job was to pull carriages in London, England. It is still popular today and has sold about 50 million copies.

What piece of horse gear was banned in 19th-century England due to outrage caused by the novel *Black Beauty*?

The bearing rein was used to keep a horse's head in an unnaturally high position while it pulled a carriage. *Black Beauty* pointed out the cruelty of the practice, and because of public outcry, the device was banned in 19th-century England. The book also inspired people to champion animal rights in general.

What horse appeared in *The Adventures of Robin Hood* starring actor Errol Flynn before becoming famous?

Roy Rogers and his horse Trigger were a famous pair in many Western movies. But before Trigger was famous in his own right, he appeared in the 1938 Errol Flynn movie *The Adventures of Robin Hood*. He was ridden by Maid Marion (played by Olivia De Havilland) and credited at the time as Golden Cloud. Roy Rogers purchased and renamed Trigger and appeared with the stallion in dozens of movies and TV shows. Trigger was born somewhere between 1932 and 1934. He was smart and able to perform many tricks, including rearing on command and walking 50 feet on his hind legs. The famous horse even had stunt doubles (named Little Trigger and Allen's Golden Zephyr). Trigger passed away in 1965 and was put on display at the

Roy Rogers–Dale Evans Museum—taxidermied (stuffed and mounted) in a rearing position—until the closing of the museum in 2009.

What famous novelty song from the 1940s referred to the diet of female horses, female deer, and baby sheep?

The song "Mairzy Doats" was recorded by the Merry Macs in 1944, with many other versions recorded later. The lyrics of the chorus are sung and written mostly as nonsense words: "Mairzy doats and dozy doats and liddle lamzy divey. A kiddley divey too, wouldn't you?" But later in the song, they give the translation: "Mares eat oats and does eat oats and little lambs eat ivy."

What were the names of the Lone Ranger's and Tonto's horses?

In the 1933 to 1954 radio program *The Lone Ranger* and later the 1938 movies and 1949 to 1957 television show, the Lone Ranger was a former Texas Ranger who became a mask-wearing vigilante (someone who fights injustice without being allowed to legally) after the rest of his troop of rangers was killed in a surprise attack. He and his Native American sidekick Tonto fought crime in the Old West with the help of two other partners: the Lone Ranger's horse Silver and Tonto's horse Scout. Silver was particularly known for coming to the rescue when called and getting the crime-fighting pair out of scrapes. The shows featured the famous cry, "Hi-yo, Silver. Away!"

What short story series inspired a famous sitcom about a talking horse?

In 1937, *Liberty* magazine published a short story called *The Talking Horse* by Walter Brooks. Its main characters were advertiser Wilbur Pope and his horse Ed, who it turned out could talk. Brooks wrote 16 stories all about Ed. A secretary at the Warner Brothers film and entertainment company enjoyed the stories and pitched the idea as a TV show. This became the show *Mister Ed*, which ran from 1961 to 1966.

What 1970s song was partially inspired by the legend of a horse who couldn't be caught?

The sad and haunting 1975 song "Wildfire," sung by Michael Martin Murphey and written by him and Larry Cansley, is about a ghost girl and horse who died in a blizzard. The song was in part inspired by a ghost story Murphey's grandfather told him about a horse who couldn't be caught, and after jumping over a chasm to avoid his captors, he returned as a ghost. Murphey later named one of his horses Miss Wildfire because of her fiery coloring.

What was used to make the sound of horse hooves hitting the ground in the 1975 movie *Monty Python and the Holy Grail*?

The comedic movie *Monty Python and the Holy Grail* centered on the story of King Arthur and his Knights of the Round Table, but the movie didn't have the knights actually riding horses. Instead, King Arthur and his group trotted and mimicked holding reins while a servant clapped two coconut shell halves together to make a sound similar to a horse's hooves hitting the ground.

What earlier toy was My Little Pony based on?

Before My Little Pony, toy designer Bonnie Zacherle designed My Pretty Pony for Hasbro. The original My Pretty Pony, released in 1981, was tan in color, 10 inches tall, and made of a hard material, although it did have a brushable mane and tail. My Little Pony was smaller, was made of a softer vinyl to make it more cuddly, and came in six different pastel colors like pink, lavender, yellow, light blue, and light green. The original toys, called the Mane 6, were named Blossom, Blue Belle, Butterscotch, Cotton Candy, Minty, and Snuzzle.

What inspired the creation of My Little Pony?

Bonnie Zacherle was inspired to create My Pretty Pony and My Little Pony by her memories of Knicker, a pony from Korea that her Army veterinarian father took care of when he and his family were stationed in Japan. According to her, Knicker was a chubby little pack pony that inspired the design of the popular toy horses. The My Little Pony toys came out in 1982 and are still going strong.

In what *My Little Pony* TV series is a unicorn sent to Ponyville to oversee an annual celebration?

The My Little Pony toy franchise was followed by several cartoon TV series and movies from the 1980s to recently. In the 2010 to 2020 TV series *My Little Pony: Friendship is Magic*, unicorn Twilight Sparkle is sent by Princess Celestia, ruler of Equestria, to Ponyville to oversee the Summer Sun Celebration. She also wants her shy mentee to make some friends. Twilight Sparkle meets Applejack (a pony), Fluttershy (a pegasus), Pinkie Pie (a pony), Rainbow Dash (a pegasus), Rarity (a unicorn) and others, and they team up to stop an evil prophesy from happening. Twilight Sparkle stays in Ponyville to have many more adventures with her new friends. The series episodes highlight characters, friendship and working together, and became popular with kids and adults alike.

In what themed restaurant and show venue can you see jousting?

Medieval Times Dinner and Tournament, originally opened in 1983, is a restaurant and show venue with an indoor arena that features jousting and other medieval tournament entertainment. You can see people in costumes ride horses while you eat!

What's the highest amount bid for a hand-painted Breyer model horse at auction?

Breyer Animal Creations, formerly Breyer Molding Company, has been making realistic, hand-painted model horses since 1950. In 2008, a Breyer model horse was sculpted to look like a real Andalusian stallion named Alborozo. A few thousand were made for that year's BreyerFest (an annual gathering celebrating the company's model horses), after which the company purposefully broke the mold. Breyer kept a few blank models from the mold. One of the remaining blank models was painted especially for the 2019 BreyerFest and was auctioned off at the festival for $22,000. But don't worry. You can buy less rare Breyer model horses starting at around $20.

In the Disney movie *Tangled*, what is the name of the major horse character?

In Disney's 2010 movie *Tangled* (a version of the Rapunzel story), a very smart horse with a unique and amusing personality named Maximus is one of the main characters. At first, he is hunting down Flynn Rider, another main character, but becomes a friend to Flynn, Rapunzel, and Rapunzel's pet chameleon, Pascal.

What is the name of Anna's horse in the Disney movie *Frozen*?

In the 2013 Disney animated movie *Frozen*, Elsa's sister, Anna, rides a Norwegian Fjord breed horse named Kjekk.

What other royal Norwegian Fjord horse appears in Disney's *Frozen*?

Hans, a suitor to Anna who isn't all that he seems, also rides a Norwegian Fjord horse. His horse is named Sitron.

What mythical horse-like creature does Elsa tame and ride in Disney's *Frozen 2*?

In the 2019 Disney animated film *Frozen 2*, Elsa encounters a shapeshifting water spirit called a Nokk that takes the form of a horse. It tries to drown her, but she tames the Nokk and rides it to save the day. The Nokk is an actual part of Norwegian mythology and is similar to the kelpie mentioned earlier in this chapter on page 109.

What horse is famous for his paintings?

You've now heard of a painted horse, but how about a painting horse? A Friesian horse named Justin who lives in the US in Columbus, Indiana paints on a special canvas on an easel using his mouth to hold the brush. Initially his owner noticed him drawing in the dirt with a dressage whip, and she decided to give him the tools to unleash his creative expression. His paintings have done well in exhibits and sales.

Chapter 9

You Can Lead a Horse to Water: Horse-Related Sayings

What is horsepower?

Horsepower is a measurement that expresses the power a machine used for transportation (especially a car) has compared with the power of a horse. The word comes directly from humans' longtime use of horses as the power behind the mass transportation of people and goods. It was coined by Scottish inventor James Watt, who improved the design of the steam engine in 1776. He wanted a way to explain the power of the engines that people at the time would understand; so he decided that 1 horsepower was equal to a horse lifting 550 pounds 1 foot into the air by pulley per second.

What is a "dog and pony show"?

The term "dog and pony show" originated in the 1800s from traveling carnivals that would include trained dogs or ponies (or both) doing tricks. Around the 1960s, it began to be used as a way to describe over-the-top events or presentations meant to distract people from a lack of substance.

What does it mean to have the "inside track"?

Having the inside track means having an advantage, especially in a competition. The term comes from horse racing, where the inner track (the one closest to the center) on the field is a shorter distance than all the other rings of the track. Therefore, a horse on the inner track has the advantage of not having to run as far.

What do people mean by "you can lead a horse to water, but you can't make it drink"?

The saying "you can lead a horse to water, but you can't make it drink" means that you can give someone an opportunity, but you can't make them take it. The earliest known appearance of a version of the phrase was in *Old English Homilies*, a collection of sayings starting from around the year 1175, during the medieval period of history. This may be the oldest English saying we still use today in some form.

What does the term "put out to pasture" mean?

When referring literally to horses, cows, sheep, and other animals who eat grass, "put out to pasture" or "put out to grass" means to bring animals to a pasture to feed. The phrase is also an expression that means to force a person out of a job and into retirement. It can also mean to stop using something, like an outdated piece of technology. "Put out to pasture" is also sometimes used to refer to animals who are retired from their jobs (like horseracing or cart pulling) to live out the rest of their lives as nonworking animals grazing in a field.

What does "horse feathers" mean?

Horses don't have feathers, just feathering hair, in some cases. You can read more about that in chapter 1, "Straight from the Horse's Mouth: Horse Terms" on page 19. But if someone responds "Horse feathers!" to something you've said, it means they think you are speaking nonsense.

What does "moving on to greener pastures" mean?

When a group of horses or other grass-eating animals eat all the grass in one area, they must travel to another that still has grass (a greener pasture) to continue feeding. When used as an expression, "moving on to greener pastures" means going to a better situation, like getting a nicer house or a better job.

What is meant by "put the cart before the horse"?

"Put the cart before the horse" is an expression that means trying to jump ahead and skip steps that should be done first. If you start trying to build a tower out of blocks but don't have enough blocks for the whole thing, you are putting the cart before the horse. The earliest known version of the saying is from William Shakespeare's play *King Lear*. After King Lear's daughter Goneril makes a demand of her father in the play, the Fool character says, "May not an ass know when the cart draws the horse?" He means that even a fool can see that King Lear and his daughter's roles have been reversed.

What does the term "hold your horses" mean?

This phrase literally refers to preventing horses from moving, which a rider or carriage driver could do by pulling back on the reins. A similar phrase is used in Homer's *Iliad* from around 800 BCE. During a chariot race in the *Iliad*, the son of Atreus said to Antiochus to get him to slow down and avoid hitting his chariot, "Antiochus, you are driving recklessly. Reign in your horses." As an expression, "hold your horses" means to wait before you do something. It is usually used by someone trying to stop someone else from doing something. Perhaps that other person is champing at the bit. See the next entry for that definition.

What does "champing at the bit" mean?

"Champing at the bit," sometimes written "chomping at the bit," means to be impatient to start doing something. You might be champing at the bit to go to an amusement park. The term comes from horses restlessly biting on the bits put in their mouths. It is thought to have originated in horseracing circles in the 1920s.

What is the meaning of "raring to go"?

Similar to champing at the bit, "raring to go" means eager to start doing something. Sometimes said "rearing to go," the phrase's origin comes from horses' habit of rearing up on their hind legs (lifting their front legs off the ground and briefly standing only on their back legs) when they are restless. "Raring" likely came from some US accents in which "rear" sounds like "rare."

What are the origins of the saying "long in the tooth"?

As horses age, their teeth get longer, so you can actually estimate a horse's age by looking at its teeth. Calling someone "long in the tooth" is calling them old. Horse's teeth aren't really growing as they age, however. Their gums are receding and their teeth are emerging from their gums, making them look like they're growing.

What does the saying "don't look a gift horse in the mouth" mean?

Since looking in a horse's mouth is one way to find out how old it is, looking in the mouth of a horse someone has given you as a gift would be checking on the value of the gift, which is considered rude. The saying "don't look a gift horse in the mouth" means don't be ungrateful for something you've received, no matter the quality.

What does "a horse of a different color" mean?

When someone says, "That's a horse of a different color," they mean that something (usually something that has just been brought up in conversation) is a different matter entirely. Fun fact: The 1939 movie *The Wizard of Oz* featured a cart-pulling horse that changed color regularly whom its driver referred to as the horse of a different color.

What is horse sense?

Horse sense is common sense. Someone who has horse sense is thought to be sensible and practical. The term originated in the early 1800s, when horses were everywhere and most people probably had positive feelings about them.

What is a hobbyhorse?

A hobbyhorse can be something a person is interested in and refers to a lot. Literally, a hobbyhorse is a toy or costume horse, including the rocking horse, the children's toy that is a stick with a horse's head at the end that kids can use to pretend they are riding a horse, and the fake horse worn in some festivals that involve Morris dancing. Fun fact: There is an annual 'Obby 'Oss festival in Padstow in Cornwall, England, that has been held for centuries. During the festival, two people in wooden horse-like costumes trot around the town accompanied by other costumed dancers and musicians to welcome the coming of summer.

What does the term "wild horses couldn't drag me away" mean?

When a person says, "Wild horses couldn't drag me away," they mean they will not leave under any circumstance. A person can also say that wild horses couldn't drag them somewhere or make them do something. Horses are very strong creatures, so this is a strong statement of resistance. It likely came from the older phrase "wild horses couldn't draw it from me," which was a reference to a medieval torture technique to get prisoners to confess by having horses painfully stretch them. The phrase "wild horses couldn't drag me away" is also used as a lyric in the 1971 Rolling Stones song "Wild Horses."

What do people mean when they say "get off your high horse"?

"Get off your high horse" means to stop acting like you are superior to others. The phrase likely came from some medieval lords and soldiers riding large horses, actually sitting higher than other people to show off their perceived superiority.

What does "don't beat a dead horse" mean?

To beat a dead horse (or flog a dead horse) means to keep doing something without hope of any change to the outcome. In reality, you shouldn't beat a horse at all, of course. It's cruel. But if a horse is dead, hitting it will accomplish nothing. So if someone is doing something pointless, you can tell them, "Don't beat a dead horse."

What does the term wild-goose chase have to do with horses?

Today, going on a wild-goose chase means chasing after something you will never get. Just like beating a dead horse, a wild-goose chase is an effort that won't accomplish anything. It was first used in Shakespeare's play *Romeo and Juliet*, in which it actually had a slightly different meaning. In the play, Romeo and his friend Mercutio are having a battle of wits, and Mercutio compares Romeo's word play to a "wild goose chase." In this case, he's saying that he knows he can't keep up with Romeo. This was a reference not to anything involving actual geese but to a type of horse race from the Elizabethan era (from

1558 to 1603) in which a lead horse would take off and other horses would follow at a distance at intervals, which made them appear to be running in a pattern similar to the flight of geese.

What is a "one-horse town"?

A one-horse town is a very small, boring town. The phrase originated in the middle of the 1800s in the United States and likely meant a town so small that only one horse was needed.

What does the saying "don't spare the horses" mean?

The quote "Home, James, and don't spare the horses" is often attributed to Queen Victoria, although it may just be an urban legend that she said this to her driver. Carriage drivers were often referred to as James, so it may have been a more general saying. The idea of not sparing the horses means not to take their comfort into consideration while making them go fast. "Don't spare the horses" as an expression means to go somewhere or do something very quickly.

What is a horse doctor?

When used literally, horse doctor means a veterinarian who specializes in providing horses with medical care. But it is also a saying that means a doctor for humans who isn't very good at their job.

What does it mean when something has "gone the way of the horse and buggy"?

This phrase refers to something no longer in use. A buggy is a type of carriage. Horse-drawn carriages used to be a common form of transportation until the invention and spread of cars made them all but disappear. Now we use this saying to refer to other things that have fallen out of use. Ask your parents about something else that has "gone the way of the horse and buggy"!

What is a "dark horse"?

In horse racing, a dark horse is one not much is known about. Therefore, no one expects it to win a race (especially when it does win). The phrase is also used to refer to anyone in a competition or political election who is relatively unknown or is doing better than expected.

What do people mean by "eat like a horse"?

To eat like a horse is to eat a lot of food. Horses eat around 20 pounds of food a day, far more than people do (although most horses are also far larger than people).

What is meant by "straight from the horse's mouth"?

To get information straight from the horse's mouth means to get it from the source rather than from someone not involved directly. It is thought that this saying either comes from the fact that you can look at a horse's teeth to estimate its age (and can therefore get information directly out of a horse's mouth) or from the idea that you can get the best horse-race-betting tips from jockeys or horse trainers who work directly with the horses and therefore know their capabilities.

What is horseplay?

Horseplay is play that's rough and rowdy.

What Shakespearean play does the quote "A horse, a horse, my kingdom for a horse!" come from?

In William Shakespeare's play *Richard III*, the title character loses his horse in battle and makes this cry as an appeal for another horse.

Who said, "I can make a general in five minutes, but a good horse is hard to replace"?

This sentence is attributed to Abraham Lincoln, 16th president of the United States.

Who said, "No hour of life is lost that is spent in the saddle"?

This quote is attributed to Winston Churchill, prime minister of England during World War II.

What is a stalking horse?

Starting in 16th-century England, a stalking horse was a real horse trained to allow a hunter to hide behind it so the hunter could get closer to the birds he was trying to shoot. It is most often used these days to refer to either something that is meant to distract from something else or a politician who attracts votes away from one candidate to the benefit of another. The phrase is more common in Great Britain than in the US.

What is the earlier version of the phrase "enough to choke a horse"?

If you have enough to choke a horse, it means you have a large quantity of something. The earlier version of this phrase was actually "enough to choke Caligula's horse." Caligula was the emperor of ancient Rome from 37 CE to 41 CE. He had a reputation for doing things in excess, so including Caligula in the phrase was likely to emphasize the excessive quantity.

What horse-derived phrase might someone say to you if you fail at something you are trying to do and they want to encourage you?

After a failure or another disappointment, a friend might tell you to "get back on the horse" as a form of encouragement. It's an expression that means to try again. The phrase comes from what someone might do if they literally fall off a horse they are riding, which would be to stand up, dust themselves off, and get back on the horse.

What does it mean to "take the reins"?

Reins are used as a way to direct or control a horse's movements. In everyday speech, to take the reins means to take charge of something (perhaps of a company or project).

What does "see a man about a horse" mean?

The original phrase was "see a man about a dog," and its first known use was In an 1865 article in the London-based magazine *The Anti-Teapot Review* and next in a play called *Flying Scud* by Dion Boucicault in 1866. Someone said they were going to see a man about a dog if they were leaving to do something they didn't want to say out loud, like using the bathroom. The saying later evolved into going to "see a man about a horse," which has the same meaning and is now more common.

Chapter 10

A Horse of a Different Color: Bonus Horse Facts

Why did some horse owners in the late 19th and early 20th century make their horses wear hats?

Horses used to be our primary form of transportation. As such, they weren't just common in the country. They were everywhere in cities. They carried riders and pulled carriages. And when it got hot, they suffered from the effects of the heat. In the late 1800s, people in Europe and the US started putting straw hats and bonnets on horses, thinking shading their heads from the sun would keep them cooler. These hats usually had holes for their ears to poke out of, and fashionable horse hats appeared in stores. But a French study in 1909 found that horses without hats had lower body temperatures than horses wearing hats. This meant that the hats were doing more harm than good, and horse hats fell out of favor.

What horse had the longest tail ever recorded?

According to Guinness World Records, JJS Summer Breeze, a mare in Kansas, set the record in August 2007. Her tail measured an astounding 12 feet 6 inches long. Imagine dragging that much hair around.

What type of musical instruments can credit horse tails for their invention?

Instruments people play with bows, like violins and cellos, owe their existence to horses, or more specifically, horses' long tails. These instruments developed from earlier stringed instruments that players plucked. It is thought that musical bows were invented in Central Asia sometime before the year 1000. The Silk Road probably contributed to their spread. Different types of fiddles from Asia to Europe also have bridges (a part that raises the strings) whose names mean "horse." And these early bows were strung with the long tail hairs of horses. In fact, nicer bows are still strung with horsehair to this day. There is also a Mongolian bowed instrument called the horse head fiddle (or *morin khuur*) that, aside from being strung with horsehair strings, also has a carved horse head at the top.

What car models are named after horse types?

The Ford Motor Company has named several of its cars and trucks after horses, including the Mustang and the Ford Bronco. Another Ford horse car was the Pinto, which is known for sometimes exploding when rear-ended by another car. Hyundai had a car called the Pony in the 1970s and an Equus starting in the late 1990s. The Subaru Brat in the US was called the Subaru Brumby in Australia (where feral brumby horses roam in the wild). The Mitsubishi Colt became the Dodge Colt starting in the 1970s. And luxury car maker Rolls-Royce had a Camargue model from 1975 to 1986, named for a feral horse breed in Southern France. Read more about this horse in chapter 2, "It's Not Rocket Science: Horse Science and Biology," on page 26.

What hairstyle has horse origins?

To make a ponytail, a person ties back longer hair and lets it hang down from the tie. This hairstyle got its name because it makes a person's hair look like a small horse's tail.

What pony breed is named for a tree?

Sandalwood ponies are named for the sandalwood trees that grow on the islands of Sumba and Sumbawa in Indonesia (the breed's area of origin).

What Japanese pony breed goes where cars and trucks cannot?

The Hokkaido pony is used to transport people around the mountainous areas of Hokkaido Island, areas that can't be reached by cars.

In the context of horse training, what is imprinting?

The 1991 book *Imprint Training of the Newborn Foal* by a veterinarian named Robert M. Miller suggested a method of horse training that involves imprinting on the foal shortly after birth. In many animal species, including horses and even humans, babies and parents bond early on through touch. Miller's method of imprinting is for a human to hold and touch the foal, even before the mother does, so the foal forms an early bond with humans and in theory will be easier to train. There is, apparently, a chance that it can backfire and make a horse less manageable later, but the method has become widely accepted by horse breeders.

What are some of the strangest laws related to horses?

There are many strange laws on the books—and laws related to horses and other animals are no exception! Here are a few that may leave you scratching your head:

- In Brooklyn, New York, and in the state of Arizona, it is illegal for donkeys to sleep in bathtubs, and in South Carolina, you can't keep a horse in a bathtub.
- In McCallen, Texas, you can't take pictures of horses on Sunday.
- In both Hartsville, Illinois, and Wilbur, Washington, it is illegal to ride an ugly horse.

- In Burns, Oregon, you have to pay admission if you want to bring your horse into a tavern.

- In Fountain Inn, South Carolina, horses must wear pants within the city, and in Charleston, South Carolina, they must wear diapers.

- In Marshalltown, Iowa, it is illegal for a horse to eat a fire hydrant.

- In Tennessee, you aren't allowed to lasso fish while sitting atop a horse.

- And cars are not technically allowed in the city limits in Las Vegas, Nevada—because they might scare the horses!

Some other horse laws are sensible, even though they sound odd. For instance, in New York City, you are not allowed to open an umbrella near a horse—with good reason! As noted earlier in chapter 3, "Eat like a Horse: Feeding and Care," on page 47, horses scare easily, likely because they are prey animals always on the lookout for danger. New York has horse-drawn carriages and mounted police. In February 2018, a horse named Arthur freaked out when a pedestrian nearby opened and closed an umbrella. Arthur raced down the street and crashed into three cars, injuring the carriage driver and his three passengers. Arthur, who had been at the job only since January and had previously pulled a tourist carriage in Cleveland, was sent to live in the country where he made a new friend, a horse named Prince.

Conclusion

Horses have worked for our benefit, enriched our lives, and even added to our vocabulary throughout the last few thousand years. And hopefully reading about them in this book has filled your brain with newfound knowledge and given you some insight into and appreciation for our equine friends and the roles they have played in our history, and in fact still play as workers, athletes, companions, and more. Buggies have gone away, but horses are here to stay. If you encounter horses in real life, remember to be kind and patient with them. And don't stand in their kicking zone!

And there is much more to learn about these amazing creatures. If you are champing at the bit to discover more about what it takes to ride, raise, or groom horses or to find out more about their history, biology, or other horse topics, there are many resources out there. Do a Google search or go to your local public library and find some books. Happy trails!

References

"3 Hurt After Spooked Horse Goes Berserk, Hits Cars: NYPD." *NBC New York*. Last updated February 5, 2018. https://www.nbcnewyork.com/news/local /spooked-horse-hits-cars-at-nyc-intersection-3-hurt-officials-central-park /1817090.

"5 Major Types of Horses Defined." *Equine Spot*. Accessed June 3, 2022. https://www.equinespot.com/types-of-horses.html.

"6 Amazing Facts about Your Horse's Face." Fédération Équestre Internationale. January 16, 2021. https://www.fei.org/stories/lifestyle/teach-me/6-amazing -facts-about-your-horses-face.

Abel, Carmella. "What Is a Gaited Horse? Everything You Need to Know." *Equine Helper*. Accessed June 5, 2022. https://equinehelper.com/what-is-a -gaited-horse.

"Adapting to -70 Degrees in Siberia: A Tale of Yakutian Horses." University of Copenhagen. November 23, 2015. https://science.ku.dk/english/press/news /2015/adapting-to--70-degrees-in-siberia-a-tale-of-yakutian-horses.

"Airs above the Ground: Classical Dressage Movements of the Lipizzaner Stallions." PBS. April 19, 2013. https://www.pbs.org/wnet/nature/legendary -white-stallions-airs-above-the-ground-classical-dressage-movements-of -the-lipizzaner-stallions/8297.

"Aintree Grand National Ladies Day." GrandNational.org.UK. Last updated April 25, 2022. https://www.grandnational.org.uk/grand-national-ladies-day.php.

Albeck-Ripka, Livia. "Majestic Icon or Invasive Pest? A War over Australia's Wild Horses." *New York Times*. June 28, 2020. https://www.nytimes.com/2020/06 /28/world/australia/brumbies-horses-culling.html.

All the Wild Horses. Directed by Ivoh Marloh. Saint Petersburg, FL: Full Exposure Films, 2018.

"American Quarter Horse." Cavalluna. Accessed May 15, 2022. https://www
.cavalluna.com/en/backstage-more/knowledge-about-horses/horse-breeds
/american-quarter-horse.

Balter, Michael. "Cave Paintings Showed True Colors of Stone Age Horses."
Wired. November 7, 2011. https://www.wired.com/2011/11/cave-painting
-colors.

Barrett, Dr. Liz. "Intro to Horse Anatomy." *US Equestrian*. January 2017.
https://www.usef.org/learning-center/videos/intro-to-horse-anatomy.

"Befuddling Birth: The Case of the Mule's Foal." NPR. July 26, 2007. https://www
.npr.org/2007/07/26/12260255/befuddling-birth-the-case-of-the-mules-foal.

"A Beginner's Guide to Horse Hacking." *Prime Stables*. Accessed June 4, 2022.
https://www.primestables.co.uk/blog/hack-horse.

Bittel, Jason. "Hold Your Zorses." *Slate*. June 19, 2015. https://slate.com
/technology/2015/06/zonkeys-ligers-the-sad-truth-about-animal-hybrids
.html.

"Biography: Seabiscuit." PBS. Accessed June 5, 2022. https://www.pbs.org/wgbh
/americanexperience/features/seabiscuit-biography.

"Bizarre Horse Laws." *Equine Wellness*. September 17, 2014. https://
equinewellnessmagazine.com/bizarre-horse-laws.

Black, Riley. "Fossil Beast Helps Fill the Backstory of Horses, Tapirs, and Rhinos."
National Geographic. November 25, 2014. https://api.nationalgeographic
.com/distribution/public/amp/science/article/fossil-beast-helps-fill-the
-backstory-of-horses-tapirs-and-rhinos.

Blocksdorf, Katherine. "How to Calculate How Much Hay to Feed Your Horse."
The Spruce Pets. Last updated February 27, 2022. https://www.thesprucepets
.com/how-much-hay-should-you-feed-1885976.

Blocksdorf, Katherine. "How to Post the Trot." *The Spruce Pets*. Last updated
October 13, 2019. https://www.thesprucepets.com/how-to-post-the-trot
-1887042.

Blocksdorf, Katherine. "Leg Markings on Horses." *The Spruce Pets*. Last updated
September 15, 2019. https://www.thesprucepets.com/leg-markings-on-horses
-1887398.

Blocksdorf, Katherine. "The Difference between English and Western Riding."
The Spruce Pets. Last updated September 3, 2019. https://www.thesprucepets
.com/english-and-western-riding-differences-1886900.

Blocksdorf, Katherine. "What Are the Olympic Equestrian Sports?" *The Spruce
Pets*. Last updated June 30, 2021. https://www.thesprucepets.com/what-are
-the-olympic-equestrian-sports-1886888.

Bratskeir, Kate. "The Craziest Laws That Still Exist In The United States." *HuffPost*.
Last updated September 5, 2017. https://www.huffpost.com/entry/weird-laws
-in-america_n_56a264abe4b0d8cc1099e1cd/amp.

Brennan, Dan. "What is Equine Therapy and Equine-Assisted Therapy?" *WebMD*. April 9, 2021. https://www.webmd.com/mental-health/what-is-equine -therapy-equine-assisted-therapy.

Brennan, Dan. "When Does a Baby Start Walking." *WebMD*. March 12, 2021. https://www.webmd.com/baby/when-does-a-baby-start-walking#091e9c5e 8213fbd4-4-7.

"Breyer History." Breyer. Accessed February 26, 2022. https://www.breyerhorses .com/pages/breyer-history.

Britton, Bianca. "Horses Can Make Facial Expressions Just Like Humans." *CNN*. Last updated June 26, 2018. https://www.cnn.com/2018/06/26/sport/horse -facial-expressions-spt/index.html.

"Buck." *Merriam-Webster Dictionary*. Accessed June 1, 2022. https://www .merriam-webster.com/dictionary/buck.

Cambridge Dictionary, s.v. "Hold Your Horses." Accessed May 15, 2022. https://dictionary.cambridge.org/us/dictionary/english/hold-your-horses.

Cerulli, Paige. "Drum Horse: Breed Profile." *The Spruce Pets*. October 15, 2020. https://www.thesprucepets.com/drum-horse-full-profile-history-and-care -5080188.

Cleaver, Emily. "Against All Odds, England's Massive Chalk Horse Has Survived 3,000 Years." *Smithsonian Magazine*. July 6, 2017. https://www .smithsonianmag.com/history/3000-year-old-uffington-horse-looms-over -english-countryside-180963968.

"Chariot." *Encyclopaedia Britannica*. November 19, 2015. https://www.britannica .com/technology/chariot.

Church, Ben. "Air Horse One: The Wonderful World Of Equine Air Travel." *CNN*. Last updated December 9, 2019. https://www.cnn.com/travel/article/equine -air-travel-horses-winning-post-spt-intl/index.html.

Claussen, Kathleen. "How Many Horse Breeds Are There?" *WebMD*. July 7, 2021. https://pets.webmd.com/how-many-horse-breeds.

"Comanche, Survivor of the Battle of the Little Bighorn." *Atlas Obscura*. Accessed June 5, 2022. https://www.atlasobscura.com/places/comanche -survivor-battle-little-bighorn.

Curtin, Melanie. "13 English Expressions with Surprisingly Funny Origins (Including 'Spill the Beans')." *Inc*. Accessed May 15, 2022. https://www.inc.com/melanie -curtin/13-english-expressions-with-surprisingly-funny-origins-including-spill -beans.html.

Daly, Natasha. "86,000 Wild Mustangs That Roam the West Are at the Center of a Raging Controversy." *National Geographic*. July 29, 2021. https://www .nationalgeographic.com/animals/article/86000-wild-mustangs-that-roam -the-west-are-at-the-center-of-raging-controversy.

"Dark Horse." Vocabulary.com. Accessed May 11, 2022. https://www.vocabulary .com/dictionary/dark%20horse.

Deluca, Ashleigh N. "World's Toughest Horse Race Retraces Genghis Khan's Postal Route." *National Geographic*. August 7, 2014. https://www

.nationalgeographic.com/travel/article/140806-mongolia-derby-horses
-genghis-riders-adventure-race.

"Discover Pony Club." Pony Club. Accessed August 1, 2022. https://www.ponyclub
.org/Discover.aspx.

"Dog and Pony Show." Grammarist. Accessed June 3, 2022. https://grammarist
.com/idiom/dog-and-pony-show.

"Dog and Pony Show." *Merriam-Webster Dictionary*. Accessed June 3, 2022.
https://www.merriam-webster.com/dictionary/dog%20and%20pony%20
show.

Donogue, Steve. "'The Perfect Horse' Is the Perfect World War II Rescue Story."
Christian Science Monitor. August 25, 2016. https://www.csmonitor.com
/layout/set/amphtml/Books/Book-Reviews/2016/0825/The-Perfect-Horse
-is-the-perfect-World-War-II-rescue-story.

Drager, M. "Triple Crown." *Encyclopedia Britannica*. May 12, 2022. https://www
.britannica.com/sports/Triple-Crown-American-thoroughbred-horse-racing.

"Dressage." *Encyclopaedia Britannica*. November 29, 2021. https://www
.britannica.com/sports/dressage.

Drum, Michelle. "Glossary of Horse Riding Terms for Beginners." *The Farm House*.
February 11, 2021. https://www.farmhousetack.com/blogs/barn-blog/glossary
-of-horse-riding-terms-for-beginners.

Dzombak, Rebecca. "Domestic Horses' Mysterious Origins May Finally Be
Revealed." *National Geographic*. October 20, 2021. https://www
.nationalgeographic.com/animals/article/do-we-finally-know-where-horses
-evolved.

"Eadweard Muybridge." *Encyclopaedia Britannica*. May 4, 2022. https://www
.britannica.com/biography/Eadweard-Muybridge.

"English Idioms." Education First. Accessed May 15, 2022. https://www.ef.edu
/english-resources/english-idioms.

"Empire of the Horse." American Museum of Natural History. Accessed June 5,
2022. https://www.amnh.org/exhibitions/horse/how-we-shaped-horses-how
-horses-shaped-us/trade-and-transportation/empire-of-the-horse.

"Eponychium." Dictionary.com. Accessed June 4, 2022. https://www.dictionary
.com/browse/eponychium.

"Equine." *Encyclopaedia Britannica*. May 19, 2020. https://www.britannica.com
/animal/equine.

"Equinophobia (Fear of Horses)." Cleveland Clinic. Accessed May 3, 2022. https://
my.clevelandclinic.org/health/diseases/22568-equinophobia-fear-of-horses.

"Eugène Delacroix." The Art Story. Accessed August 3, 2022. https://www
.theartstory.org/amp/artist/delacroix-eugene.

Evans, Margaret. "Horses with Jobs: Barge Horses." *Horse Journals*. Last
updated February 1, 2022. https://www.horsejournals.com/popular/history
-heritage/horses-jobs-barge-horses.

"Ever Wonder Why It's Called a 'Dude Ranch?'" Colorado Trails Ranch. Accessed June 5, 2022. https://coloradotrails.com/blog/ever-wondered-why-its-called -a-dude-ranch.

"Extreme Mustang Makeover." Mustang Heritage Foundation. Accessed June 5, 2022. https://mustangheritagefoundation.org/extreme.

Fabus, Taylor. "Defining Horse Jargon: Horse Sale Terms." Michigan State University Extension. July 12, 2019. https://www.canr.msu.edu/news/defining -horse-jargon-horse-sale-terms.

"Famous Horses." Smithsonian. Accessed May 15, 2022. https://www.si.edu /spotlight/famous-horses.

Finn, Ed. "What Exactly Is a 'Stalking Horse?'" *Slate*. September 23, 2003. https:// slate.com/news-and-politics/2003/09/what-exactly-is-a-stalking-horse.html.

"Flora Temple." Smithsonian. Accessed February 5, 2022. https://www.si.edu /object/flora-temple:nmah_325827.

Fought, Emily. "10 Silly Horse Laws That Surprisingly Exist." *Cowgirl Magazine*. September 13, 2019. https://cowgirlmagazine.com/silly-horse-laws.

Fought, Emily. "English vs Western: What Is Right for You?" *Cowgirl Magazine*. December 1, 2017. https://cowgirlmagazine.com/english-vs-western.

Fought, Emily. "The Largest and Smallest Horse Breeds." *Cowgirl Magazine*. March 15, 2019. https://cowgirlmagazine.com/largest-smallest-horse-breeds.

Fought, Emily. "Whoa! Have You Ever Seen 'Foal Slippers?'" *Cowgirl Magazine*. April 20, 2021. https://cowgirlmagazine.com/foal-slippers.

Foy, Peter. "What's a Knokk? Everything You Need To Know About Frozen 2's Water Horse." CBR. November 22, 2019. https://www.cbr.com/frozen-2-nokk -guide.

Free, Cathy. "World's Tallest Dog Is 7 Feet on Hind Legs. He Likes to Sit on Laps." *Washington Post*. May 12, 2022. https://www.washingtonpost.com/lifestyle /2022/05/12/zeus-tallest-dog-guinness-records.

Freeberg, Ernest. "The Horse Flu Epidemic That Brought 19th-Century America to a Stop." *Smithsonian Magazine*. December 4, 2020. https://www .smithsonianmag.com/history/how-horse-flu-epidemic-brought-19th-century -america-stop-180976453.

Garo, Shahan. "The Mongol Pony Express." *TLDR History*. Accessed June 5, 2022. https://tldrhistory.com/2020/05/26/the-mongol-pony-express/amp.

"George Stubbs, British, 1724–1806." National Gallery of Art. Accessed June 3, 2022. https://www.nga.gov/collection/artist-info.1912.html.

"Gift horse." Vocabulary.com. Accessed May 15, 2022. https://www.vocabulary .com/dictionary/gift%20horse.

"A Glossary of Equine Vocalizations." *Horse Illustrated*. Accessed May 17, 2022. https://www.horseillustrated.com/horse-keeping-a-glossary-of-equine -vocalizations/amp.

"A Glossary for Horse Tack." Transwest. Accessed May 18, 2022. https://www .transwest.com/horse-livestock-trailers/blog/a-glossary-for-horse-tack.

Grame, Theodore C. "Stringed Instrument." *Encyclopaedia Britannica*, January 29, 2019. https://www.britannica.com/art/stringed-instrument.

Grigg, Gordon, Fritz Geiser, Stewart Nicol, and Dr. Christopher Turbill. "Not Just Sleep: All about Hibernation." Science.org. Accessed February 26, 2022. https://www.science.org.au/curious/hibernation.

GrrlScientist. "Almost All Modern Horses Descended from a Few Oriental Stallions." *Forbes*. July 10, 2017. https://www.forbes.com/sites/grrlscientist /2017/07/10/almost-all-modern-horses-descended-from-a-few-oriental -stallions/?sh=6fc3734f16c5.

"The Hagerman Horse (Equus simplicidens)." National Park Service. Accessed May 14, 2022. https://www.nps.gov/articles/000/equus_simplicidens.htm.

"Hambletonian Stakes." *Encyclopaedia Britannica*. July 31, 2018. https://www .britannica.com/sports/Hambletonian-Stakes.

"Hand." *Encyclopaedia Britannica*. June 14, 2007. https://www.britannica.com /science/hand-measurement.

"Hansom can." *Encyclopaedia Britannica*. February 9, 2018. https://www .britannica.com/technology/hansom-cab.

Harris, James C. "Chauvet Cave: Panel of Horses." *Arch Gen Psychiatry* 68, no. 9 (2011): 869–870. https://jamanetwork.com/journals/jamapsychiatry /fullarticle/1107262.

Hasbro. "My Little Pony—The Original Mane 6." Accessed February 26, 2022. https://mylittlepony.hasbro.com/en-us/characters/retro-ponies.

"High horse." Vocabulary.com. Accessed May 15, 2022. https://www.vocabulary .com/dictionary/high%20horse.

"History of the Horseshoe." American Equus. Accessed June 5, 2022. https:// americanequus.com/history-of-horeshoes.

"History of Jousting." *History UK*. Accessed May 19, 2022. https://www.history .co.uk/article/history-of-jousting.

"History of the Polo Shirt." *Polo Weekly*. Accessed June 5, 2022. https:// poloweekly.com/history-of-the-polo-shirt.

Hobbyhorse Revolution. Directed by Selma Vilhunen. Pottstown, PA: MVD Visual, 2018.

Homer. *Iliad—Book XXIII*. Translated by Samuel Butler. Accessed May 15, 2022. http://classics.mit.edu/Homer/iliad.23.xxiii.html.

"Hoof." *Kids Britannica*. Accessed June 4, 2022. https://kids.britannica.com/kids /article/hoof/400115#.

"Horse." *National Geographic*. June 10, 2011. https://www.nationalgeographic .com/animals/mammals/facts/horse.

"A Horse of a Different Color." *Merriam-Webster Dictionary*. Accessed May 15, 2022. https://www.merriam-webster.com/dictionary/a%20horse%20of%20 a%20different%20color.

Horse & Hound. "Canine Teeth in Horses: All You Need to Know." June 23, 2004. https://www.horseandhound.co.uk/horse-care/horse-care-tips/canine-teeth -in-horses-56093.

"A Horse of a Different Color: Common Equine Coat Colors!" ASPCA. May 6, 2021. https://www.aspca.org/news/horse-different-color-common-equine-coat-colors.

"Horse-Story in the Making: The Budweiser Clydesdales." Anheuser-Busch. November 21, 2016. https://www.anheuser-busch.com/about/clydesdale.

"Horse Doctor." *Merriam-Webster Dictionary.* Accessed May 15, 2022. https://www.merriam-webster.com/dictionary/horse%20doctor.

"Horse Sense." *Merriam-Webster Dictionary.* Accessed May 15, 2022. https://www.dictionary.com/browse/horse-sense.

"The Horses of Eugene Delacroix." The Equinist. Accessed August 3, 2022. http://www.theequinest.com/horses-of-eugene-delacroix.

"Horseshoe." *Encyclopaedia Britannica.* February 21, 2012. https://www.britannica.com/topic/horseshoe.

"Horse Trekking vs Hacking—What Is the Difference?" Fir Tree Farm Equestrian Centre. Accessed July 30, 2022. https://www.firtreeequestriancentre.co.uk/activities/horse-trekking-vs-hacking-what-is-the-difference/#iLightbox[gallery2161]/0.

Humane Society of the United States. "The Rules of Feeding Your Horse." Accessed May 3, 2022. https://www.humanesociety.org/resources/rules-feeding-your-horse.

IMDb. "My Little Pony: Friendship is Magic (2010–2020)." Accessed August 3, 2022. https://m.imdb.com/title/tt1751105.

IMDb. "Seabiscuit (1939)." Accessed June 1, 2022. https://m.imdb.com/title/tt0384511.

IMDb. "Seabiscuit (2003)." Accessed June 1 , 2022. https://m.imdb.com/title/tt0329575.

IMDb. "The Story of Seabiscuit (1949)." Accessed June 1, 2022. https://m.imdb.com/title/tt0041923.

Innes, Emma. "The Father of ALL Racehorses: Scientists Discover Majority of Modern Thoroughbreds Are Descended from the British Stallion Eclipse." *Daily Mail.* April 5, 2013. https://www.dailymail.co.uk/sciencetech/article-2304521/The-Adam-equine-world-Scientists-discover-Thoroughbreds-descended-stallion-Eclipse.html.

"Inside Track." Grammarist. Accessed August 1, 2022. https://grammarist.com/idiom/inside-track.

Integracare. "Lame Horse—Causes, Symptoms & Cures of Equine Lameness." October 28, 2021. https://integricare.ca/blog/lame-horse.

International Brotherhood of Teamsters. "The Early Years." Accessed June 4, 2022. https://teamster.org/about/teamster-history/the-early-years.

International Olympic Committee. "The Sports Events." Accessed June 1, 2022. https://olympics.com/ioc/ancient-olympic-games/the-sports-events.

Italiano, Laura. "Runaway Carriage Horse Makes New Friend, Becomes Symbol for Animal Activists." *New York Post.* February 9, 2018. https://nypost.com

/2018/02/09/runaway-carriage-horse-makes-new-friend-becomes-symbol-for-animal-activists/amp.

Jensen, Karen. "How General Patton and Some Unlikely Allies Saved Austria's Fabled White Horses." HistoryNet. September 18, 2009. https://www.historynet.com/patton-saves-austrias-white-horses.

Johnson, Ben. "The Kelpie." *Historic UK*. Accessed April 24, 2022. https://www.historic-uk.com/CultureUK/The-Kelpie.

Jones, Meghan. "Here's Where Your Favorite Animal Related Sayings Come From." *Reader's Digest*. Last updated March 7, 2022. https://www.rd.com/list/where-animal-sayings-come-from.

Joseph Filippi Winery. "The Mini Stallions of Regina Winery." Accessed June 4, 2022. https://josephfilippiwinery.com/history.

Kane, Callan. "The Smallest Horse in the World." *Cowgirl*. January 29, 2015. https://cowgirlmagazine.com/the-smallest-horse-in-the-world.

Kentucky Equine Research Staff. "Don't Flake Out: Feed Horse Hay by Weight, Not by Flake." September 16, 2015. https://ker.com/equinews/dont-flake-feed-horse-hay-weight-not-flake.

Klimek, Kim. "What's the Difference between a Paint Horse and a Pinto?" *Horse Illustrated*. 2020. Accessed May 20, 2022. https://www.horseillustrated.com/horse-exclusives-paint-vs-pinto/amp.

"Lady Suffolk." Harness Racing Museum and Hall of Fame. Accessed February 20, 2022. https://harnessmuseum.com/content/lady-suffolk.

Laliberte, Marissa. "Jousting Rings True as an Exercise in Precision, Focus and Camaraderie." *Baltimore Sun*. September 27, 2014. https://www.baltimoresun.com/sports/bs-sp-outdoors-jousting-0928-20140927-story.html.

"The Life and Times of Figure." National Museum of the Morgan Horse. Accessed June 5, 2022. http://www.morganmuseum.org/html/figure.html.

"The Lipizzaner Stallions." Visiting Vienna. Accessed May 29, 2022. https://www.visitingvienna.com/sights/lipizzaner.

"Lone Ranger." *Encyclopedia Britannica*. June 7, 2015. https://www.britannica.com/topic/Lone-Ranger.

Marques, Andreia. "7 Biggest Horses & Horse Breeds in the World." *Horsey Hooves*. Last updated February 28, 2021. https://horseyhooves.com/biggest-horse-breeds.

Marques, Andreia. "How Much Does a Horse Weigh?" *Horsey Hooves*. Last updated July 17, 2021. https://horseyhooves.com/how-much-does-a-horse-weigh.

Maudlin, Lauren. "The Breyer Model Horse That Sold for $22,000." *The Plaid Horse*. July 23, 2019. https://www.theplaidhorse.com/2019/07/23/the-breyer-model-horse-that-sold-for-22000.

Maxwell, Noelle. "Secret History: The Fascinating Story of Nautical, a Palomino Show Jumper with a Golden Career." *Horse Nation*. July 2, 2014. https://www.horsenation.com/2014/07/02/secret-history-the-fascinating-story-of-nautical-a-palimino-show-jumper-with-a-golden-career.

Maxwell, Noelle. "'Unbridled Abstract Expressionistic': Justin the Artistic Horse." *Horse Nation*. March 21, 2019. https://www.horsenation.com/2019/03/21 /unbridled-abstract-expressionistic-justin-the-artistic-horse.

McClure, Robert C. "Functional Anatomy of the Horse Foot." University of Missouri Extension. Accessed May 30, 2022. https://extension.missouri.edu /publications/g2740.

McGraw, Eliza. "Why Horses Used To Wear Bonnets, Caps and Peaked Straw Hats." *The Washington Post*. August 1, 2017. https://www.washingtonpost.com /news/animalia/wp/2017/08/01/why-horses-used-to-wear-bonnets-caps -and-peaked-straw-hats.

Meier, Allison. "Taxidermists Restore Napoléon's Beloved White Horse." *Hyperallergic*. July 12, 2016. https://hyperallergic.com/310371/taxidermists -restore-napoleons-beloved-white-horse.

Memmott, Mark. "Chew on This: Is it Chomping or Champing?" NPR. June 9, 2016. https://www.npr.org/sections/memmos/2016/06/09/605796769/chew-on-this -is-it-chomping-or-champing.

MeTV Staff. "Horse Around with These 14 Fascinating Facts About 'Mister Ed.'" MeTV. July 29, 2016. https://www.metv.com/lists/horse-around-with-these-14 -fascinating-facts-about-mister-ed.

Milbert, Neil. "'Tanto's Pacer' Ever Faithful." *Chicago Tribune*. November 17, 1994. https://www.chicagotribune.com/news/ct-xpm-1994-11-17-9411170221-story .html.

Mill, Andrea. *Everything Book of Horses and Ponies*. London: DK Publishing, 2019.

"Mairzy Doats." Lyrics.com. Accessed May 11, 2022. https://www.lyrics.com/lyric /3629230/The+Merry+Macs/Mairzy+Doats.

Miller, Kelli. "Saliva and Your Mouth." *WebMD*. Accessed April 24, 2022. https:// www.webmd.com/oral-health/what-is-saliva.

Mohr, Melissa. "Are Horses 'Rearing to Go' or 'Raring to Go?'" *Christian Science Monitor*. July 23, 2020. https://www.csmonitor.com/The-Culture/In-a-Word /2020/0723/Are-horses-rearing-to-go-or-raring-to-go.

Monaco, Pete. "Beautiful Jim Key and the Former Slave Who Taught Him to Count and Use the Alphabet." *The Spectrum*. March 25, 2019. https://www .thespectrum.com/story/sports/mesquite/2019/03/25/beautiful-jim-key -worlds-smartest-horse-and-owner-william-key/3267109002.

Monger, Helen. "Joseph Hansom and the Hansom Cab." *Historic UK*. Accessed June 5, 2022. https://www.historic-uk.com/HistoryUK/HistoryofBritain/Joseph -Hansom-the-Hansom-Cab.

"Morgan." *Encyclopaedia Britannica*. August 1, 2013. https://www.britannica.com /animal/Morgan-horse.

Morton, Ella. "The Surprising Resurgence of Side Saddle." *Slate*. April 12, 2016. https://slate.com/human-interest/2016/04/the-surprising-resurgence-of-side -saddle.html.

Munroe, Randall. "How Fast Can a Human Run?" *New York Times*. Last updated February 7, 2020. https://www.nytimes.com/2020/01/21/science/human-running-speed-quadruped.html.

Nix, Elizabeth. "Did Caligula Really Make His Horse a Consul?" *History*. August 30, 2018. https://www.history.com/news/did-caligula-really-make-his-horse-a-consul.

NOAA. "Glacial-Interglacial Cycles." National Oceanic and Atmospheric Administration. Accessed February 24, 2022. https://www.ncei.noaa.gov/sites/default/files/2021-11/1%20Glacial-Interglacial%20Cycles-Final-OCT%202021.pdf.

Nogrady, Bianca. "Scientists Say Australian Plan to Cull Up to 10,000 Wild Horses Doesn't Go Far Enough." *Nature*. November 1, 2021. https://www.nature.com/articles/d41586-021-02977-7.

O'Brien, Anna. "Why Turnout Is Important for Your Horse." *The Spruce Pets*. Last updated December 23, 2021. https://www.thesprucepets.com/importance-of-turnout-for-your-horse-1886932.

Olivet Nazarene University. "The United States of Crazy Laws." Accessed May 4, 2022. https://online.olivet.edu/news/united-states-crazy-laws.

"One-horse town." Dictionary.com. Accessed May 15, 2022. https://www.dictionary.com/browse/one-horse-town.

"The Original Mr. Ed, The Talking Horse: A Compilation of 16 Stories—Walter Brooks." Archive. July 27, 2018. https://archive.org/details/brookswalthertheoriginalmr.edthetalkinghorse16stories/page/n1/mode/2up.

"Over the Fence: George the Unicorn." *Horse Illustrated*. Accessed June 5, 2022. https://www.horseillustrated.com/over-the-fence-blog-2015-0409-george-the-unicorn/amp.

"Padstow's 'Obby 'Oss Festival Returns after Two Years." *BBC News*. May 2, 2022. https://www.bbc.com/news/uk-england-cornwall-61296744.

Page, George. *Nature*. Season 37, Episode 8, "Equus: Story of the Horse Part 1: Origins." Aired January 16, 2019, PBS. PBS Documentaries channel, Amazon Prime.

Page, George. *Nature*. Season 37, Episode 9, "Equus: Story of the Horse Part 2: Chasing the Wind." Aired January 23, 2019, PBS. PBS Documentaries channel, Amazon Prime.

Paulson, Dave. "Story Behind the Song: 'Wildfire' by Michael Martin Murphey." *The Tennessean*. June 28, 2019. https://www.tennessean.com/story/entertainment/music/story-behind-the-song/2019/06/28/wildfire-michael-martin-murphey-story-behind-song-horse-cowboy-country-music/1570277001.

Paulick Report Staff. "Brain Size Matters: Are Horses Smarter Than Humans?" December 28, 2017. https://paulickreport.com/horse-care-category/brain-size-matters-horses-smarter-humans.

Pavia, Audrey. *Horses for Dummies: 3rd Edition*. New Jersey: John Wiley & Sons, Inc., 2020.

"Permanent exhibition: Messel Pit." Senckenberg Museum Frankfurt. Accessed February 5, 2022. https://museumfrankfurt.senckenberg.de/en/exhibition /permanent-exhibitions/messel-pit.

"Pinto." *Encyclopaedia Britannica*. January 21, 2018. https://www.britannica.com /animal/Pinto-type-of-horse.

Podhajsky, Alois Wilhelm and E. Gus Cothran. "Horse." *Encyclopaedia Britannica*, May 3, 2021. https://www.britannica.com/animal/horse.

"Pony." *Encyclopaedia Britannica*. June 4, 2013. https://www.britannica.com /animal/pony.

"Prohibition." *History*. Accessed June 5, 2022. https://www.history.com.amp /topics/roaring-twenties/prohibition.

Price, Michael. "Most Modern Horses Came from Just Two Ancient Lineages." *Science*. June 29, 2017. https://www.science.org/content/article/most-modern -horses-came-just-two-ancient-lineages.

"Przewalski's Horse." *National Geographic*. March 12, 2010. https://www .nationalgeographic.com/animals/mammals/facts/przewalskis-horse.

"Przewalski's Horse." Smithsonian's National Zoo & Conservation Biology Institute. Accessed February 24, 2022. https://nationalzoo.si.edu/animals /przewalskis-horse.

"Put the Cart before the Horse." *Merriam-Webster Dictionary*. https://www .merriam-webster.com/dictionary/put%20the%20cart%20before%20the%20 horse.

"Put Out to Pasture." *Merriam-Webster Dictionary*. Accessed May 15, 2022. https://www.merriam-webster.com/dictionary/put%20out%20to%20pasture.

"Q&A: Why Can't Horses Vomit?" *Equus Magazine*. July 26, 2021. https:// equusmagazine.com/horse-care/qa-horses-vomit-28006.

"Rustling." *Collins Dictionary*. Accessed May 29, 2022. https://www .collinsdictionary.com/us/dictionary/english/rustling.

Rattenbury, R. C. and Russell, Don. "Rodeo." *Encyclopedia Britannica*, February 27, 2020. https://www.britannica.com/sports/rodeo-sport.

"The Real Definition of Impulsion in Dressage." *Wehorse*. December 16, 2019. https://www.wehorse.com/en/blog/impulsion-dressage-horse.

Redrup, Gemma. "29 Fascinating Facts About Horses (That You Will Struggle To Believe Are True...)." *Horse & Hound*. January 14, 2022. https://www .horseandhound.co.uk/features/horse-facts-653825.

Reeve, Moira C. and Sharon Biggs. *The Original Horse Bible—2nd Edition*. Mount Joy, PA: CompanionHouse Books, 2021.

Rizzo, Katherine O. "Jousting: Maryland's State Sport for 50 Years." *Equiery*. July 17, 2018. https://equiery.com/jousting-marylands-state-sport-for-50-years.

Ronan, Amanda Uechi. "Someone Named Kikkuli Was the First Horse Trainer." *Horse Nation*. July 27, 2015. https://www.horsenation.com/2015/07/27 /someone-named-kikkuli-was-the-first-horse-trainer.

Ronan, Amanda Uechi. "What the Muck Is That? Eponychium." *Horse Nation*. March 26, 2016. https://www.horsenation.com/2016/03/21/what-the-muck-is -that-eponychium.

Rosenberg, Zoe, and Amy Plitt. "Inside the Luxury Digs That the NYPD's Horses Call Home." *Curbed New York*. June 1, 2017. https://ny.curbed.com/2017/6/1 /15721774/nypd-mounted-unit-stables-mercedes-house.

"Ruminant." *Encyclopaedia Britannica*. June 25, 2021. https://www.britannica .com/animal/ruminant.

Rutherford, David. "10 Facts about the Horsehair on a String Player's Bow." *CPR Classical*. April 21, 2014. https://www.cpr.org/2014/04/21/10-facts-about-the -horsehair-on-a-string-players-bow.

Salopek, Paul. "Rediscovering China's Ancient Tea Horse Road, a Branch of the Famous Silk Road." *National Geographic*. March 21, 2022. https://api. nationalgeographic.com/distribution/public/amp/history/article/rediscovering -chinas-tea-horse-road-a-branch-of-the-silk-road.

Shakespeare, William. *King Lear*, Act 1, Scene 4. https://shakespeare.folger.edu /shakespeares-works/king-lear/act-1-scene-4.

"Shetland Pony." *Encyclopaedia Britannica*. February 1, 2018. https://www .britannica.com/animal/Shetland-pony.

"The Silk Road." Khan Academy. Accessed May 14, 2022. https://www .khanacademy.org/humanities/world-history/ancient-medieval/silk-road/a /the-silk-road.

Silver, Madeleine. "15 of the Greatest Horse Quotes of All Time (from Churchill to Shakespeare)." *Horse & Hound*. October 4, 2021. https://www.horseandhound .co.uk/features/best-horse-quotes-of-all-time-637724.

Smith, James. "The History of the Polo Shirt from Rene Lacoste through Ralph Lauren." *Heddels*. April 15, 2019. https://www.heddels.com/2019/04/history -polo-shirt-rene-lacoste-ralph-lauren.

"Stalking horse." Dictionary.com. Accessed May 14, 2022. https://www.dictionary .com/browse/stalking-horse.

Stanek, Anna. "6 Types of Mustang Horses & Their History." *Horsey Hooves*. Last updated May 2, 2021. https://horseyhooves.com/types-of-mustang-horses.

Stanek, Anna. "7 Interesting Facts about Trigger, Roy Rogers' Horse." *Horsey Hooves*. Last updated November 22, 2021. https://horseyhooves.com/trigger -roy-rogers-horse.

Stanek, Anna. "10 Amazing Horse Statues and Sculptures in the World." *Horsey Hooves*. Last updated September 9, 2020. https://horseyhooves.com/horse -statues-sculptures.

Stanek, Anna. "14 Best Horse Documentaries." *Horsey Hooves*. Last updated April 15, 2021. https://horseyhooves.com/horse-documentaries.

Stanek, Anna. "Chincoteague Wild Ponies of Assateague Island." *Horsey Hooves*. Last updated February 8, 2022. https://horseyhooves.com/chincoteague -ponies.

Stanek, Anna. "List of Every Disney Horse (Description, Film & Owners." *Horsey Hooves*. Last updated May 14, 2022. https://horseyhooves.com/disney-horse.

Stanek, Anna. "Top 10 Mythical Horses & Their Mythology." *Horsey Hooves*. Last updated April 22, 2021. https://horseyhooves.com/mythical-horses.

"Steam Engine." *Encyclopaedia Britannica*. May 28, 2020. https://www.britannica.com/technology/steam-engine.

Stevens, Erica. "What Is a Hunter Pace?" Equine Welfare Society. Last updated October 3, 2019. https://www.equinewelfaresociety.org/post/what-is-a-hunter-pace.

"Studbook." *Encyclopaedia Britannica*. February 15, 2011. https://www.britannica.com/science/studbook.

"Suffolk." *Encyclopaedia Britannica*. January 8, 2018. https://www.britannica.com/animal/Suffolk-horse.

Suetonius. *The Lives of the Twelve Caesars*. Translated by Alexander Thomson, MD. Revised by T. Forester, Esq., AM. Project Gutenberg. Last updated August 31, 2016. https://www.gutenberg.org/files/6400/6400-h/6400-h.htm#link2H_4_0005.

Szathmary, Henrietta. "7 Medieval Warhorse Breeds." *Horsey Hooves*. Last updated February 14, 2021. https://horseyhooves.com/medieval-war-horse-breeds.

Szathmary, Henrietta. "20 Horse Idioms and Sayings Explained." *Horsey Hooves*. Last updated December 5, 2021. https://horseyhooves.com/horse-idioms.

"Tallest Horse Ever." Guinness World Records. Accessed July 31, 2022. https://www.guinnessworldrecords.com/world-records/70453-tallest-horse-ever.

Taylor, William. "Pandemics and the Post: Mongolia's Pony Express." *The Diplomat*. October 16, 2020. https://thediplomat.com/2020/10/pandemics-and-the-post-mongolias-pony-express.

"Teamster." Vocabulary.com. Accessed June 4, 2022. https://www.vocabulary.com/dictionary/teamster.

"Tennessee Walking Horse." *Encyclopaedia Britannica*. November 7, 2016. https://www.britannica.com/animal/Tennessee-walking-horse.

"Texas Rangers." *Encyclopaedia Britannica*. August 31, 2021. https://www.britannica.com/topic/Texas-Rangers-United-States-military-force.

"Three-Day Event." *Encyclopaedia Britannica*. September 9, 2009. https://www.britannica.com/sports/three-day-event.

"Thoroughbred." *Encyclopaedia Britannica*. June 22, 2017. https://www.britannica.com/animal/Thoroughbred.

"Top 11 Cars Named After Horses, Which Is Your Favorite?" ClassicCars.com. May 8, 2021. https://journal.classiccars.com/2021/05/08/top-11-cars-named-after-horses-which-is-your-favorite.

Trentin, Summer and Debbie Sneed. "Alexander and Bucephalus." University of Colorado. June 19, 2018. https://www.colorado.edu/classics/2018/06/19/alexander-and-bucephalus.

Trimble, Marshall. "Hitching Posts." *True West Magazine*. December 13, 2019. https://truewestmagazine.com/hitching-post.

Tréguer, Pascal. "Meaning and Origin of the Phrase 'to See a Man about a Dog.'" *Word Histories*. Accessed May 15, 2022. https://wordhistories.net/2017/11/09/see-man-about-dog/amp.

Turner, Zeke. "Riding a Hobbyhorse: Yes, It's an Organized Sport." *Wall Street Journal*. March 28, 2017. https://www.wsj.com/articles/best-in-sew-inside-the-growing-sport-of-hobbyhorse-riding-1490713811.

"Understanding Your Horse's Brain." *Horse Illustrated*. Accessed June 4, 2022. https://www.horseillustrated.com/your-horses-brain/amp.

"Ungulate." *Encyclopaedia Britannica*. February 12, 2021. https://www.britannica.com/animal/ungulate.

University of Texas at Austin. "Eye Size Determined by Maximum Running Speed in Mammals." *ScienceDaily*. May 2, 2012. https://www.sciencedaily.com/releases/2012/05/120502112606.htm.

"US Horse Population—Statistics." American Horse Council. June 10, 2020. https://www.horsecouncil.org/press-releases/us-horse-population-statistics.

Wallenfeldt, Jeff. "Pony Express." *Encyclopaedia Britannica*, April 11, 2016. https://www.britannica.com/topic/Pony-Express.

"What Is a Steeplechase?" Racing Explained. Accessed June 5, 2022. https://www.racingexplained.co.uk/jump-racing/what-is-a-steeplechase.

"What Is Horsepower and Why Is It Important?" Toyota Canada. July 25, 2019. https://www.toyota.ca/toyota/en/connect/3887/what-is-horsepower.

"'Wild Goose Chase,' Meaning and Context." No Sweat Shakespeare. Accessed May 15, 2022. https://nosweatshakespeare.com/quotes/famous/wild-goose-chase.

"Wild horses couldn't drag me." Dictionary.com. Accessed May 15, 2022. https://www.dictionary.com/browse/wild-horses-couldn-t-drag-me.

"Wild West show." *Encyclopaedia Britannica*. May 27, 2010. https://www.britannica.com/art/Wild-West-show.

Williams, Paige. "The Remarkable Comeback of Przewalski's Horse." *Smithsonian Magazine*. December 2016. https://www.smithsonianmag.com/science-nature/remarkable-comeback-przewalski-horse-180961142.

Wood, Craig. "How a Horse's Hoof Grows." *Extension Horses*. January 22, 2020. https://horses.extension.org/how-a-horses-hoof-grows.

Wright, Tony. "Black Beauty Taught Us Long Ago to Treat Horses Kindly. What Happened?" *The Sydney Morning Herald*. November 7, 2019. https://www.smh.com.au/national/black-beauty-taught-us-long-ago-to-treat-horses-kindly-what-happened-20191107-p538a6.html.

Xenophon. "On Horsemanship." Gutenberg.org. Accessed February 26, 2022. https://www.gutenberg.org/files/1176/1176-h/1176-h.htm.

About the Author

Bernadette "Berni" Johnson began her writing career at age 6 when she crayoned a book about her mom that received a rave review from its only reader. One of her much more recent published works is *The Big Book of Spy Trivia*.

When Berni's not watching movies or fiddling with a computer, she studies history, science, and other fun stuff, reads and writes fiction and nonfiction, and does the bidding of her little terrier. You can read her blog and find links to her writing at bernijohnson.com.

9 781646 044474